Swing Trading

A Beginner's Guide to Options Trading Strategies, Money Management, and Market Psychology. Why you should Step Out of your Comfort Zone to Be Successful in Stock Market Investing

when it comes to the recounting of facts. As such, any use, correct or incorrect, of the provided information will render the Publisher free of responsibility as to the actions taken outside of their direct purview. Regardless, there are zero scenarios where the original author or the Publisher can be deemed liable in any fashion for any damages or hardships that may result from any of the information discussed herein. Additionally, the information in the following pages is intended only for informational purposes and should thus be thought of as universal. As befitting its nature, it is presented without assurance regarding its prolonged validity or interim quality. Trademarks that are mentioned are done without written consent and can in no way be considered an endorsement from the trademark holder.

Table of Contents

Chapter 6: Money Management 131

Conclusion 151

Introduction

Congratulations on purchasing *Swing Trading,* and thank you for doing so.

The following chapters will discuss different aspects of swing trading. The first chapters will introduce you to trading and why you need to start trading today. People have been trading the markets and earning large sums of money regularly. You too, can begin earning huge profits and live the kind of life you have always desired.

The book introduces you to the stock markets and the basics of swing trading. You will learn why swing trading is the strategy of choice and how it enables you to earn a passive income as you go about your day attending to your everyday matters.

You will also learn how to take profits, how to re-enter the markets, and how to automate your trades so that you are free to do other things. Risk management and money management are crucial aspects of trading. This book takes you slowly through these important subjects so that you are ready to begin trading within the shortest time possible.

There are plenty of books on this subject on the market, thanks again for choosing this one! Every effort was made to ensure it is full of as much useful information as possible; please enjoy it!

Chapter 1: The Stock Markets

The stock markets, also known as the equities markets, are markets where traders buy and sell stocks of publicly traded companies. Stocks consist of different kinds of shares, the most common being ordinary shares.

Stock Markets are like Auctions

It is easy to view stock markets as auctions where traders buy and sell stocks to the highest bidders. Shares are ownership units of publicly-traded companies. Companies often sell their shares to the public as a revenue-raising venture. Investors and even traders purchase these shares in order to benefit from future profits and also trade them when the prices go up.

Stock markets are also secondary markets where both sellers and buyers, retail and institutional, gather to trade in shares. These markets are regulated by governments and overseen by organizations such as stock exchanges. There are a number of stock exchanges around the world. Some of the most popular ones are JPX or the Japan Exchange Group, the New York Stock Exchange or NYSE, and the London Stock Exchange or LSE.

At the stock markets, we have retail traders, institutional investors, individual traders, and also public companies. Institutional investors are professionals who trade on behalf of large organizations such as banks. It also includes financial organizations and investment firms like hedge funds and retirement schemes.

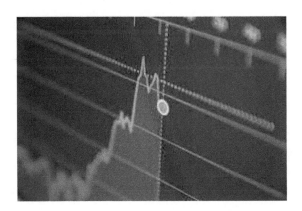

Listing at the Stock Markets

Companies usually list at the stock market to seek funding. Publicly listed companies are generally companies whose finances are in order and have a sound business plan. Before listing, they have to prove their success, profitability, and long-term plans to the regulator. Regulators assess companies over a period of time, say three years or so before allowing them to list at the stock exchange.

The reason behind this is simple. First, investors put their money in companies in the hope that these companies will perform well and earn a profit, which will then be shared among shareholders. Non-profitable companies can result in losses, and investors will feel like they invested in losing companies. Losing money at the bourse, while not unheard of, is not what investors seek. It is the duty of the regulator to set standards and regulate the markets to protect investors and traders as well as maintain high standards as required by law.

A company that intends to list at the stock markets will issue what is known as an IPO or initial public offer. This means selling shares to the public for the very first time. A privately-owned company that lists at the bourse ceases to be one and instead becomes a public company. This is because there are now new shareholders who are also part-owners of the company. They will be able to influence company policy, share in dividend distribution, and so much more. However, investors do not have to hold onto the shares forever. They are free to sell them to other investors or traders at the stock exchange.

Companies that list at the stock market not only gain much-needed funds but also get to raise their profiles. They become better known and well respected in their respective industries and in financial circles. They use the money they receive to make capital investments such as acquisition of land, property, or even buying out other businesses. Companies also use the funds to expand into new ventures, modernize their equipment, and generally grow their operations.

They will acquire certain obligations such as annual auditing of accounts and releasing this information publicly as well as calling shareholder meetings and paying out dividends. In return, their shares will trade at the stock exchanges, and they will gain in value over time.

Traders love strong companies with large volumes. In fact, most traders at the stock markets always lookout for large, blue-chip companies with large volumes and are profitable. They prefer these companies because they are liquid and hence, easier to acquire and dispose of shares. These are just some of the features that traders and investors look for in companies. Those with smaller volumes and very little activity pose a challenge.

Making Money with Stocks

Once an investor invests their money in shares at the stock markets, they can use them to make money in one of two different ways. The first one is to sell the shares when the prices go up. This is bound to happen sooner or later because stock prices are always going up and sometimes falling. Savvy traders make a living through selling and buying of shares on a regular basis. This can be quite profitable for those with the necessary skills and stock market understanding. Such profits are referred to as capital gains.

Apart from capital gains, investors can also make money through dividend payments. Companies often pay out dividends to shareholders. Sometimes this happens once a year and sometimes biannually. Therefore, stock investors earn through capital gains or dividends and sometimes even both.

Listed companies announce profits and then allocate some of that profit to shareholders. This amount is often paid out to shareholders depending on the type and number of shares held. Some shareholders will always get paid whether a company is profitable or not. Others will be paid depending on the company's financial performance.

There is generally a minimum amount that you can expect to receive annually. There are many companies that do not pay a dividend annually. Many others have the reputation of having paid dividends to shareholders over a long period of time.

Equity Derivatives and Short Positions

There is another avenue for shareholders to make money through their shares. These are equity derivatives and short positions. There are a number of crucial factors that determine a stock's value. These include a company's intrinsic value, demand, supply, interest rate, economic factors, and so on.

Other Ways of Investing at the Stock Market

You can invest in seven different ways in the stock market. Online purchase and sale of stocks are one of the easiest and most convenient ways. It is important to learn a little bit more about how the stock market works, how to buy shares, how to sell, and so on. This book will teach you all that you need to know about shares and stocks and how to buy and sell at the stock market.

The stock market consists of a number of exchanges. These include NASDAQ, the New York Stock Exchange, and others. It is here that stocks and other financial instruments like bonds are registered.

Important Points to Note

At this point, we understand that the stock market is where we buy, sell, and trade in stocks. There are a host of other financial securities that are traded here too. They include indexes, funds, bonds, and so on. However, the most popular of these instruments are stocks.

One of the best ways of earning a residue income is through stock market investing. We do this by purchasing appropriate stocks at the stock market. You can learn how to choose stocks for investment and trading purposes. It is pretty easy and straightforward. However, some people prefer letting brokers do this for them. Brokers charge for their services, but their advice is solid and reliable.

More About Stocks

Stocks carry a price because they can be sold or bought at the secondary markets. This price is based on a number of factors, including the company's earnings. Positive news such as good financial performance, expansion, renowned CEO, and so on often has an effect on the price, which is mostly positive. When the company performs poorly, then the stock price is likely to fall. Therefore, the price of stocks depends on factors such as a company's profits, the general performance of the economy, and positive news regarding the company. Negative news affects the company's stock negatively.

Initial Public Offering of Shares or IPO

Companies seeking funding usually open up to the public by selling shares at the stock exchange. By selling shares to the public, they become a public company, and others get to own a part of the firm. In return, they receive large sums of money, which they can use for different uses. For instance, funds can be used for expansion, for infrastructure acquisition, and sometimes for branching out into new markets or new ventures.

When shares are sold to the public for the very first time, the process is referred to as the initial public offer or IPO. IPO stocks are often very lucrative because the prices are likely to increase significantly upon listing.

Buying Stocks

The processor mechanics of purchasing and selling stocks is standard. As an investor, you first need to obtain a stock quote. This is information that lets you know the types of shares available, the quantity, and the current price. Such information can help you to make the correct buy decisions.

Now, once you know what is available in the market, you will then have to place an order. There are 2 basic types of orders. These are the limit order and the market order.

Market order: this is an order that you place if you wish to buy a particular share immediately and at the best possible price. Here, you will be guaranteed of the order's immediate execution. With a market order, you will buy shares at a price closest to the posted ask price. The same is true if you wish to sell shares. Your shares will sell at the market at a price closest to the nearest posted bid. This is a great way, as an individual trader to get your orders executed immediately. You may not know the exact price, but you can expect to pay or receive a price as close to the bid or ask price as possible.

Limit order: This is an order that sets both the maximum and minimum prices that you are willing to pay for or sell your shares. However, there are always commissions involved, and they are usually higher for limit orders but lower for market orders.

Terms Commonly Used at Stock Markets

If you are to successfully invest in the stock market, then you need to be familiar with common trading terminology. These are pretty basic but necessary if you are to be successful. Here is a look at a couple of definitions.

ASK Price: This is the lowest price that a stock owner is willing to sell his shares. Shares and stocks are also known as financial securities. If you own stock that you wish to sell, then the asking price is the lowest minimum amount that you can accept.

BID Price: The bid price is the largest price that a buyer will accept to pay for stocks or shares. As a buyer, you will have to agree on this price.

Bear: The term bear refers to an investor whose opinion is that a particular stock or the entire market will fall in the coming days or weeks. A bear market is one where stock prices are in decline.

Bull: A bull market is one where the prices are rising, and the general market is performing positively.

Broker: A broker acts as an agent. This is a person or firm that sells and buys stocks and other securities on behalf of a client. In return, the broker is paid a fee. This fee is known as a commission.

Book Value: This is the net value of a company when all its liabilities are deducted from the assets.

Profits/Earnings: This refers to the profit made by a company in the course of one financial year. The profit is what remains after all other expenses such as taxes and overheads are paid. A profitable company is said to be "in the black" while that which is losing money is said to be "in the red." Profits are also referred to as the Bottom Line.

Dividends: The term dividend refers to an amount of money that is set aside from the profits for onward payment to shareholders. Therefore, whenever a listed company makes a profit, a portion of it should be paid out to shareholders. This is done in the form of dividend payments.

Income/ Sales/ Revenue: These terms are different from profits and a company's bottom line. It refers to money earned as a result of the sale of goods and products it produces or from the service it provides.

Market Capitalization: This term, sometimes referred to as market cap, indicates the value of a company by its traded shares. Market capitalization is determined by multiplying the number of outstanding shares with the current share price.

Dow Jones Industrial Average: The DJIA is a widely used index that measures the performance of the US Stock Market. It is very popular with traders because its performance points to the performance of most other shares. The Dow Jones Industrial Average consists of weighted stocks from 30 Blue Chip companies.

Mutual Funds: A mutual fund is simply an investment company that pools together money from different investors and then invests this money on different financial securities such as stocks at the stock exchange.

Securities: This term, in the context of financial investments, translates to bank deposits, bonds, and stocks. You can purchase and sell securities at the stock markets.

Spread: This essentially refers to the difference in price between Bid and Ask.

Equities / Stocks: A company's capital is divided into shares, and when shares are put together, they constitute stocks. 100 shares = 1 stock as stocks are purchased in bundles of 100. A person who owns company stock basically owns part of that company. There is usually physical or digital evidence of ownership.

Volume: In finance, volume refers to the sum total of all shares traded on any given trading day.

Yield: Companies pay dividends to their shareholders either annually or biannually. Yield is the percentage of the dividend in comparison to share price. For example, if the share price is $10 and the dividend payout per share is $0.50, then the yield, in this case, is 0.5/10 % = 5%.

Speculation Versus Investing

Sometimes stock market experts use the terms speculation and investment synonymously because of certain similarities. However, there are certain features that distinguish one from the other. These demarcation lines are crucial if investors are to clearly differentiate one term from the other.

Investment: An investment could be the purchase of a financial asset such as stocks with the hope of a future price rise and hence, profitability. A trader or investor spends their funds buying financial security, hoping it will generate good returns in the shortest time possible.

Speculation: This is when a trader or investor invests their funds in financial security, but this time with a certain level of risk. Speculation aims to generate profits in a short period of time while investments are spread out over a long period of time.

Most investors spend money on financial assets and stock market securities in the hope that their efforts will be profitable in due course. Investing means spending money based on reasonable judgments and within acceptable risk levels. For instance, before buying shares, an investor should consider a number of factors, including past performance, the status of the economy, analysis, and other forms of due diligence. Such an approach is very likely to succeed.

In situations where a person engages in undertakings that are very likely to flop and without any foundations such as fundamental and technical analysis, then this is referred to as speculation.

Investing comes in a variety of ways. In the world of stock markets and investing, it refers to the purchase and sale of securities such as bonds, stocks, currencies, and futures. There is quite a variety of financial instruments to choose from. The aim, in this case, is to profit from or generate an income from the expected returns on the investment through capital gains.

Income is also derived from dividends paid out by listed companies to shareholders. However, investing is a long-term venture where investors purchase securities and hold for a relatively long period of time. Holding and waiting is a common strategy used by investors. Think about an individual trying to raise capital to start his or her business or perhaps a down payment for a home. Such an individual can buy and hold stocks or other financial markets securities. After a period of perhaps five years, the investment may have grown significantly.

Sometimes investors also hope to earn a regular income over a period of time. They will invest in stocks or bonds and then receive a regular income through both capital gains and regular dividend payouts. Investing can be a continuous process where regular amounts are added onto an existing investment over a period of time. This grows the investment and provides an opportunity for immense growth over time.

Different Types of Stock Trading

When you begin trading stocks, you will be buying and later selling the stocks in order to realize a profit. There are different ways that you can achieve this. First, you will need to find a broker and sign up with them. Once this process is done, you will fund your account with investment capital and then begin the stock buying process.

Before buying shares, you will need to learn how to trade, including common terminology used by traders. After learning all the basics, you will also need to learn the different types of stock trading. There are about nine different trading types. These are also known as active types of trading where a trader engages in active trading at the stock market.

Day Trading

This strategy involves trading in securities and closing out trades or exiting within the same day. This means you first identify a suitable stock using fundamental analysis as well as all the tools in your possession, including charts.

You will first enter a trade then be on the lookout for small but significant price movements. Day trading tries to take advantage of particular events that are likely to have an impact on the price movement of a particular stock. For instance, stocks become volatile and usually experience an upward direction during earnings announcements. Another significant event includes financial announcements by the regulator, as these announcements may directly impact stocks and shares.

Swing Trading

Another popular active trading strategy is swing trading. This strategy involves entering a position and holding it for a while. The time variable in this instance varies from a couple of hours to a couple of weeks. However, on average, this amount is usually between a single day and two weeks.

This approach is less stressful and allows traders to make more profits with longer price movements. For instance, as a trader, you will buy stocks and then leave the trade to play out its course. You could as such, be working for one company but also trading during your free time. Swing traders also make great profits, especially when riding the momentum and trade in large volumes. Most traders prefer this strategy because of its approach to trading.

Scalping

Scalping is the least popular trading strategy, yet it is still great for trading profitably. This particular strategy makes use of small price movements in the markets to earn a profit. You will never hold a position for a long time as the strategy here calls for fast entry and fast exist.

A lot of the time, scraping happens at the stock market when there is plenty of leverage available. For instance, there could be a share or stock that is expected to rise drastically. If you apply this trade, then you will need to take stock of all stocks before actually buying so as to determine the market conditions as well as prices indicated on minute charts and tick charts.

Position Trading

This is yet another popular stock trading type for short-term trading. It is very similar in some aspects to both intra-day and swing trading. Basically, a position trader is a trader who assumes a position in a financial asset or stock market instrument but for a long period of time.

Position traders are also viewed as investors because of the length of time they remain in their positions. Investors generally buy and hold positions for lengthy periods of time. Position traders come really close to this. They hold positions for a couple of weeks and sometimes even months. They are the best contrast to day traders who assume positions in the market for only a day. Day traders never hold overnight positions.

More About Active Trading

As a trader, you will engage in active trading in highly liquid markets searching for profitable opportunities based on price movements on certain stocks and shares. The most commonly traded securities are stocks, even though there is a wider option available.

As a trader, you will need to be a lot more speculative compared to the average investor, which leads us to the use of fundamental and technical analysis. Technical analysis will come in handy when you plan your trades. You will also require additional tools, including price charts, which are crucial tools for any active trader.

You will need to make a lot of trades if you are to be profitable. High trade volumes are recommended with volatility. As a trader, you should find volatile stocks with large volumes and plenty of price movement. The reason why you should deal in high volume stocks is that price movements are often small, so to maximize profits, large volumes are necessary.

Another important aspect of active trading includes the regular application of limit orders. These orders enable you the trader to determine and set stock prices ideal for selling your stocks. As a trader, you need to plan your trades so that you know when to take profits and what points to exit a trade. To exit a non-performing trade, you will need to define stop-loss points.

A stop-loss order is an order that you come with to prevent your trades from losing your money. A typical stop-loss order identifies a price point located at a lower position on the trend. Should the price fall to the stop-loss point, then you will automatically exit the trade and prevent further loss of funds. This point is considered the maximum loss that you can take per trade. It is advisable to take this approach as you risk letting your emotions get the better of you.

Costs Affiliated with Active Trading

There are certain costs inherent with active trading strategies. These costs include commissions, fees, and other costs charged by brokerage firms. There are also software and hardware requirements necessary for the implementation of these setups and strategies. Apart from that, we have other needs, such as access to real-time market data and similar trading information. However, these costs are considered a necessary aspect of trading and are enablers of successful trading at the securities markets.

Applying trading strategies correctly will ensure that you are profitable, which implies that these costs will easily be recouped.

Chapter 2: Swing Trading Basics

There are different trading styles used by traders. Styles are chosen mostly depending on preferences as well as goals. Seasoned stock market traders are able to choose a trading style depending on the market conditions and their projections. Some seasons demand one particular trading style, while other seasons demand different styles of trade.

Out of the numerous trading styles in common use, swing trading is among the most popular. This is because it does not consume a lot of time, the strategy is simple enough to understand, and it can be very profitable. It is also not as intense as others or as risky as some strategies.

What is Swing Trading?

Swing trading is a stock trading strategy where a trader buys and holds stocks for a relatively short period of time. In fact, most strategies are similar; the only difference is the amount of time spent holding a position. Swing traders hold stocks for a period that ranges between a few days to a couple of weeks. The minimum amount of time is at least a day, while the longest is often two months. As such, swing traders are said to lie between position traders and day traders.

Position traders enter a position and hold it for weeks and sometimes even months. On the other hand, day traders enter positions and exit before the end of the day. As such, swing traders who hold positions at least overnight lie between these two. It is a strategy best suited for trading stocks and options. As a swing trader, you will on average endeavor to make money each week. If you can enjoy returns ranging from 10% to 20%, then you will enjoy attractive returns and a profitable run at the markets.

How to Approach Swing Trading

Swing trading is a relatively simple strategy. However, hard work is determining a couple of initial factors. For instance, you have to learn how to choose the right stocks. There are numerous stocks listed at the stock market, but not all are suitable for trading purposes.

You also need to learn how to undertake analysis. Fundamental analysis is crucial in determining the worth of a company as well as the real value of its stock. We also have a technical analysis. It is useful in determining entry points, exit points, and expected performance. If you learn how to do your due diligence, then you will be able to trade with little or no worry. In return, you will also make attractive returns on a regular basis. Earning a passive income on a regular basis without too much hard work is definitely an important achievement.

Reasons for Swing Trading

The main aim of swing trading is to find the major trend and then apply swing trading strategies to the trend in order to earn profits and make big wins. As a swing trader, you will hold either a short or long position in the marketing often for a minimum of 2 days to probably 2 weeks.

This time frame is not exact because some trades conclude pretty fast, while others may last for a few months. Even in such rare instances, the strategy is still considered to be swing trade. Your aim in all instances will be to profit from large price movements.

There are some swing traders who prefer less volatile and more sedate financial instruments, while others opt for very volatile ones. In both instances, a trader will try to identify the direction of an asset's price before moving in and eventually cashing in on the profit made from the price movement. Successful swing traders aim to benefit from large chunks of the desired price movement before proceeding to the next available chance.

Swing trading has proven to be among the most preferred forms of trading and making money. It is important to ensure that your technical analysis skills are up to scratch if you are to trade and be profitable consistently. You will also be assessing trades based on a risk versus reward ratio. This is done using charts. Chart analysis will help you to determine where to enter a trade, when to exit and where to take profits. As a swing trader, you will mostly rely on the 15-minute or 1-hour charts to determine the most suitable stop loss and entry points.

Apart from technical analysis, you will also need to ensure that your fundamental analysis skills are up to scratch. For instance, you may notice that a stock is on an upward trend, and you want to get and benefit from its movement. Before doing so, you will need to confirm that its fundamentals are sound and secure.

As a trader, you can risk about $1 in order to make $3. This is considered a reasonable and favorable risk to reward level. However, risking $1 to make perhaps $1 or less is considered unfavorable.

Swing Trading Tips

Swing traders prefer dealing in multiple-day rather than single-day charts. Common chart patterns that are favored by swing traders include triangles, flags, head and shoulder patterns, cup, and handle patterns, as well as the moving average crossovers. However, each trader is expected to come up with their own trading strategy that suits their purpose, style, demeanor, and so on.

The best approach is to identify and come up with a strategy that provides one with an edge over numerous other trades. To come up with such a trade, a trader will need to identify suitable trade setups that point towards predictable movements of the chosen asset. Achieving such a feat is never easy, and even the best strategies do fail some of the time.

No trader is victorious on each trade. Even the most successful and well-known traders such as Warren Buffet lose out one some trades. All you need is to identify a suitable and favorable risk versus reward ratio. In fact, to be profitable, you will only require a very favorable risk to reward ratio without the need to be successful in all your trades.

Trends

The market trend is the market's response to the rising and falling of prices of listed securities. When the market is on an upward trend, it implies rising prices and increased value of listed securities. Such a market is known as a bullish market, and the trend is said to be bullish. On the other hand, a downward trend implies falling stock prices due to factors such as tough economy, high-interest rates, and other factors. Such a market is said to be bearish, and the trend is also a bearish one.

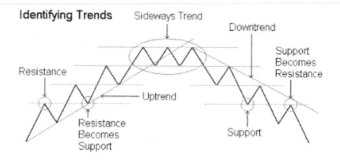

How to Identify Market Trends

There are generally three kinds of trends. These are short-term, medium, and long-term trends. As a trader, you can expect to encounter any one of these trends as you carry out your due diligence, especially technical analysis. There is a lot that new traders need to learn about the trend. One of these is that the trend is always on your side. As much as possible, make sure that you follow it. Always follow the trend, and you will be right almost all the time. Going against the trend is considered an exercise in futility.

One of the first lessons any trader needs to learn is to identify the trend and its direction. This is done using technical analysis. Technical analysis is a form of analysis used by traders to determine a couple of important factors about a trade, including

37

the trend, trading volumes, the ideal stock to trade, entry points, and exit points.

Primary Markets

Bull markets and bear markets are considered as primary markets. Markets are bullish most of the time. However, each bullish period is often followed by a bear market. Statistics show that these markets have a duration lasting between one and three years.

On the other hand, we also have what is known as a secular trend. Basically, a secular trend is one that consists of numerous primary trends and can last anywhere from a decade to a couple of decades, sometimes up to thirty.

Intermediate Trends

We also have intermediate trends. These occur and are visible in primary trends. When intermediate trends occur, they tend to puzzle both traders as well as business journalists who try to find answers about factors that cause intermediate trends.

An intermediate trend appears suddenly and causes the trend to head in the opposite direction for seemingly no apparent reason. Directional turnarounds and sudden rallies are the main cause of intermediate trends and usually the outcome of some sort of political or economic activities as well as any subsequent reaction.

According to history, intermediate rallies that occur in bull markets are generally stronger compared to those occurring in bear markets. However, the reactions are basically weak. In bear markets, the reactions are generally strong, but any rallies are brief and do not last long. There are usually three different intermediate cycles in each bear or bull market. A single cycle can last as long as 6 weeks to 8 months or as little as 2 weeks.

In short, we can conclude that stock markets consist of a number of different trends. As a trader, you need to be able to note and observe these trends because your success or otherwise at the markets will depend on your ability to recognize them.

Different Financial Instruments

When it comes to trading the markets, most traders typically opt for stocks even though they have numerous alternatives to choose for. Additional financial instruments include other types of stocks, currencies, indexes, crypto-currencies, options, futures, and so on.

If you are a beginner, then it is best to start with stocks. These are pretty easy to trade, and transactions are rather straightforward. Also, most of the trading information available largely refers to stock trading. Once you become proficient in stocks, then you will gain sufficient experience to begin trading with other securities. Here is a look at some of these financial instruments.

Stocks

Stocks are the most common type of security that you are likely to come across. These are traded at the stock market, which is a secondary market. Owners or holders of stocks usually trade with willing buyers on a regular basis at the stock exchange. On most occasions, if not all, you will be buying or trading in stocks with other interested participants but not the parent company.

Every stock comes with a quote. This quote is never fixed but varies depending on a number of factors. Prices are not the only information provided. We also have other information available relating to stocks. For instance, traders are interested in volumes traded as volume is a great indicator of liquidity.

The prices of stocks are often determined through an auction process at the stock exchange. Buyers and sellers basically place bids and offers, and when they coincide, a sale is concluded. If you wish to buy stocks, you will visit your broker, who will place bids on your behalf. Alternatively, you can open an online account and do so via a trading platform. Most transactions have moved online, making it easier and more convenient to trade in stocks and shares.

There are different kinds of orders found in the stock market. For instance, we have limit orders and market orders. A market order is where a client uses an online platform or instructs a broker to sell or buy stocks at the best price possible. Market orders never guarantee the price that you want, but you will almost certainly get the number of shares desired.

Limit order simply means an all or none order. In this instance, when you place an order, it will only be fulfilled if you receive the entire amount of shares that you desire. For instance, if you wish to purchase 500 shares of stock ABC, then this AON or all-or-none order will only be fulfilled if the 500 shares are available. If the supply falls short, then the order will not be fulfilled.

We also have short selling and margin trading. Margin refers to a loan provided by a broker for trading purposes. When you engage in margin trading, it simply means that you are purchasing stocks using borrowed funds. The same is true when it comes to shares or stocks that do not belong to you. When you sell short, it means that you are selling shares that belong to someone else.

Both margin and short selling are popular with traders. The purpose is always to sell or buy with the aim of buying back or selling with the aim of profiting from the venture. At the same time, you will trade with the hope of returning borrowed stocks or repaying the margin loan.

Currencies

Currencies from across the world are traded at the Forex markets. In fact, the Forex market is the most liquid market. The reason for this is that all transactions are opened and closed using cash, and trades are concluded instantly. There are trillions of dollars in circulation each day with traders located in countries all around the world. The most amazing part is that there are no central authorities that oversee the Forex market. This is a self-regulating market. It consists of a network of individual traders, banks, other institutions, and brokers. All trades are executed via banks and brokers.

If you wish to trade in currencies, then you will first have to learn how to trade. Once you are confident about your trading skills, you can then begin trading. The Forex markets are accessible and every single business day 24 hours a day throughout the year. Sometimes Forex trading is available even during the holidays when it is made available in other jurisdictions. For instance, there may be a US national holiday such as Memorial Day. Currency trading may still be available through other countries where they do not have a similar holiday.

There are numerous companies that deal in Forex. Such companies often trade with clients or customers overseas. Currency fluctuations affect their businesses, especially when they buy or sell products and services. Hedging against currency options is one way of countering the challenge posed by fluctuations. This is achievable through Forex markets.

Forex is traded in pairs and offered as a quote. Currency pairs' examples include USD/JPY, CAD/AUS, and so on. A quote that is offered on a currency pair refers to the ratio of the value of one currency against the other. For instance, if we have the currency pair USD/CAD quoted as 1.2569, then it means that one US dollar has a value equivalent to 1.2569 CAD. As such, it costs 1.2569 CAD to buy 1 USD. These values are never static but dynamic and constantly changing because of different reasons.

Trading the Forex markets is easy and straight forward. It is very similar to trading stocks. The only difference, in this case, is the financial instrument. If you can trade stocks, then you should be able to adjust to trading Forex because the principle is the same. When you trade Forex, you are actually buying currencies. It is exactly what a tourist from France, for instance, would do with their euros in the US. They would exchange them for US dollars.

Indexes

An index is basically a measure or indicator of a certain parameter. When it comes to finance, the index refers to a measure of change in a given market. We have stocks, shares, and bonds as securities traded in the financial markets. Some of the popular indexes in the US include the S&P 500 as well as the DJIA or Dow Jones Industrial Average. We also have others, such as the US Aggregate Bond Index. These are often used to benchmark the performance of the US bonds and stock markets, and these are measures of the US economy.

A Closer Look at Indexes

There are different indexes and each related directly to either bonds or stock markets. Also, each index has a specific calculation formula. Usually, the numeric value of an index is not as important as the relative change of the index. The most crucial part to investors is often the total amount an index has fallen or risen with a period of time, like 24 hours for instance.

Indexes have a base level of 1,000. However, investors and traders are often interested in the variation of the index from this base level. For instance, if the FTSE 100 has a value of 7643.50, then we can see that it is almost 8 times larger than the base level. As a trader, you need to be on the lookout for the percentage drop or rise of an index.

There is a certain close relationship between exchange-traded funds, mutual funds, and trading indices. Fund managers usually try to mirror certain indexes when they constitute exchange-traded funds and mutual funds. For instance, a fund manager will observe and note all the stocks that constitute a popular index such as the Dow Jones Industrial Average and then mirror that with their fund. This way, the fund will be expected to perform in tandem with the index. Should the index appreciate in value then the fund will also gain in value.

Because funds such as these mirror major indexes, investors are able to invest in securities contained in an index. The performance of ETFs – electronically traded funds – and mutual funds is often measured by the performance of indexes. Thus, they act as benchmarks for investors and traders in most cases. A mutual or ETF fund can compare its returns to that of the S&P 500. This way, investors are able to compare how their fund is performing and whether they are profiting or not in relation to the fund.

One of the most popular indices is the S&P 500 or Standard & Poor's 500. This index is commonly and popularly used by traders, fund managers, investors, and other market players to benchmark the stock market. This index constitutes three-quarters or approximately 75% of all the stocks and securities trades across the US.

Another very popular index is the DJIA or the Dow Jones Industrial Average. It is well known, but the only challenge is that it reflects only a small percentage of the stocks traded in the US stock markets. The Dow Jones consists of stocks of no more than 30 companies traded at the stock exchanges. Apart from the DJIA and S&P 500, other notable indexes are Wilshire 5000, NASDAQ, and the Barclays Capital Aggregate Bond Index.

Index funds have been created to enable us to invest indirectly in indexes. We have index funds that track the performance of certain select stocks. A good example of an ETF is the Vanguard S&P 500. It consists of lots of securities that are similar to those found on the S&P 500.

We also have mortgage index funds. ARMs or the Adjustable-Rate Mortgages constitute adjustable interest rates that last throughout the lifetime of the mortgage. This rate is basically determined through the use of a margin that is added to an index. A good example of an ARM is LIBOR or London Interbank Offer Rate. To determine the interest on a loan, all you need to do is determine the LIBOR rate and mortgage index to the LIBOR. If the former is 3% and the latter is 2% then the interest rate on a mortgage is 3% - 2% = 1%.

Options

Options are a versatile product for trade and investment. They can be defined as derivative contracts where buys have a right but not obligation to purchase underlying security. The underlying security is usually priced at an agreed amount. While the buyer of an option is under no obligation to buy the underlying security, the seller is always obligated to sell should the buyer exercise their right.

Both investors and traders sell and buy options. Sometimes investors and business owners buy options for hedging purposes. This means that they buy options to reduce their risks regarding exposure. However, most traders and investors sell and buy options to generate an income, earn a profit, growth their investments, and so on.

Options trading can be very lucrative because profitability is exponential, unlike with other instruments. You could easily make over ten or even twenty times of your capital with just a single trade. However, options are also a very risky prospect. A lot of traders lose money trying to trade options. Ensure that you only do so if you are skilled, experienced, and have a sure trading plan.

When you sell options, you get to earn fees. Writing options can be a simple way of making an income. There is also the advantage of leverage when trading options, as well as protection of a portfolio by hedging. Therefore, trading options can be very rewarding and fulfilling.

E.T.F.s or Exchange-Traded Funds

ETFs or exchange-traded funds are largely associated with growth investing and index tracking. However, there are ETFs that do provide an income through purchase and ownership of dividend-paying stocks. These are stocks that pay dividends regularly. When these are received by the ETF, they are then distributed equitably to all members.

Also, bonds earn interest each month, but it is not paid out until bond maturity. As such, I bonds are said to be zero-coupon bonds. The interest is compounded twice a year. Payment is on a fixed rate basis, and inflation is factored into the payment. Any interest earned is exempt from taxation at both local and state levels. However, some federal taxes do apply when the bonds mature or are redeemed.

Order Flows

The term order flow refers to a trading concept. It is the order flow that ensures that market prices are never constant but always on the move. In fact, numerous traders make decisions based on a number of factors, such as order flows. Such moves are referred to as order flow trading which is also known as order flow analysis.

Traders and investors generally place orders at the stock markets. These are orders to either purchase or sell securities and are placed through brokers. In return, the brokers are paid a fee, which is usually a single penny per share. This payment is compensation to brokers for placing orders with different third parties.

The most important aspect of order flow is the nature of compensation. Third parties basically compensate brokers who send orders their way for fulfillment. This kind of deal is also great for small brokerage firms that are unable to handle numerous orders on their own. They get to share out some of their orders to third parties, and in return, they receive payment out of it.

The law requires that you be notified should your broker outsource your trades to another broker. This is supposed to happen at least once a year. Therefore, you should check with your broker and find out if there are any orders that were outsourced to third parties.

The Market Rhythm

Traders believe that rhythm is important. For instance, each year has different seasons, such as winter and spring. Our lives also have rhythm. We encounter highs and lows in life, and these give life real and true meaning. In the same manner, we also enjoy rhythm when it comes to music and so much more.

The stock markets also possess some rhythm. If you want to be a successful trader, then you need to learn the market rhythm and feel it. Traders generally need to be in sync with the beat and soul of the market.

Market Swings

The market is constantly in motion. A swing occurs when there are two consecutive lower highs and lower lows or when there are two consecutive higher lows and higher highs. Remember that swings appear in all manner of shapes and sizes. However, the rule on how to identify them is very simple. Simply look for consecutive higher highs and higher lows or consecutive lower highs and lower lows.

Swings are bullish if the general movement is upwards and bearish if the general movement is downwards. Sometimes a new low will appear when the trend is upwards. At other times a new high will appear when the general trend is headed downwards. When this happens, you should not be worried or concerned as these are considered false swings. Unless there are consecutive highs or lows, then ignore everything else.

Use Swings to Increase Profitability

We have learned how to identify swings in the market. Now we need to apply this knowledge in order to be profitable. The first step is to place your stop-loss points. This should be slightly above the higher high for a bearish situation and below the lowest low in a bullish situation.

Also, the correct and accurate swing highs and swing lows provide an opportunity to draw Fibonacci extensions. These lines will enable you to identify target areas of high probability. As such, it becomes possible to place our take profit and stop loss points on our charts. Remember Livermore? The gentleman said to be one of the most successful traders ever? Back in 19 29, he managed to make about $100 million. In today's terms, this is equivalent to almost $1.4 billion. That is a lot of money, even for an experienced trader.

If you learn about the best trading systems, then you, too, can make plenty of money in today's prevailing marketing rates. You could always trade with the market trend or against it. Remember that it is always advisable to follow the trend rather than the opposite. Only oppose the trend if you are an experienced swing trader and know exactly what you are doing. Key will be identifying the best entry points into a trade and the best places to collect profits as well as exit trades.

Before you begin your swing trading ventures, ensure that you come up with a tested plan that you can implement. Therefore, test your preferred systems and strategies and ensure that they are working as desired. This way, you will be able to prepare appropriately and trade successfully and profitably over time.

Swing traders are always searching for conditions in the markets where stock prices are looking to swing either downwards or possibly upwards. There are numerous technical indicators that are available to enhance your trades. Indicators used in swing trading are basically essential in identifying trends in the market between certain trading periods.

These trading periods that range anywhere from 3 to 15 are then analyzed using our technical indicators in order to determine the presence or otherwise of resistance and support levels. If these have actually materialized and are clearly visible, then we can proceed to make other determinations.

At this stage, you will also need to determine whether any trend is bullish or bearish. You will also need to be on the lookout for a reversal because without one; you will not be able to enter a trade. Reversals are also referred to as countertrends or pullbacks. As soon as we can clearly point out the reversal, then we can easily identify the appropriate entry point.

The entry point should be the point where the pullback is just about to come to an end, and the trend is about to pick up again. Being able to determine these points is really crucial. This same approach is the very same one used by Jesse Livermore to earn his wealth.

Find Best Stocks for Trading

One of the most crucial things that you need to do in order to be a successful swing trader is to correctly identify ideal stocks or other financial instruments to trade. The first step in identifying ideal stocks is to identify obvious catalysts. A catalyst is an event that can cause a stock price to increase exponentially within a short time period.

Think about events such as economic data points, regulatory announcements, earnings reports, and other scheduled events that can impact the world of finance. Most of these events are predictable and known way ahead of time. Due to this predictability, you are able to know when to keep track of events, get ready, and eventually get into the market. Most swing traders are able to time these events perfectly and proceed to benefit from stock price movements.

In the United States, for instance, traders already know that on the first Tuesday of each month, the auto industry will release their sales figures. The strength of the sales will help determine whether the stocks will trend upwards or downwards. Major auto companies in the US include Ford Motor Company, General Motors, and Fiat Chrysler, among others.

Another thing you have to be on the lookout for is volatility. Volatility is your friend as a swing trader. You should be wary of long upward or downward trends as they provide no clear exit or entry points. However, some volatility will come in handy. When there is some volatility, then you will clearly see the best spots to place a stop-loss and profit-take points, as well as entry and trade exit points.

Swing trading can be challenging before you get used to it. Most of the time, you will be working with different tools trying to make the best of prevailing market conditions. One of the benefits of swing trading over day trading is that you will mostly be saving your trading capital through buying and holding for a couple of days.

However, there are some challenges related to stock hoarding for days or weeks at a time. One of these challenges includes events and news that occur overnight. However, even with these risks, you are still able to find a suitable stock to trade.

There are three basic approaches used to determine the most appropriate stock depending on your preferred trading style. These are technical analysis, major events or catalysts, and fundamental analysis. You can choose your preferred style to begin your hunt for an ideal stock.

Initial Steps

The first thing you need to do is find out if there are any major events expected to happen. These are events that will have a direct impact on stock prices, for example, earnings reports. It is important to do this because not only are these events predictable, but they provide an excellent chance for any serious swing trader.

There are a couple of places to check for events. The internet is one such place. Search the internet for upcoming events in the world of finance and sometimes even politics. Political announcements sometimes affect business in a huge way. One of the best websites to check out is www.earningswhispers.com. Others include www.finviz.com, Bloomberg, and CNBC. Most seasoned swing traders also favor the SEC filings websites where they can search for companies that have filed returns.

You will also need to use technical analysis. This is essential if you are to find some potential trades. Technical analysis also comes in handy when there is a known catalyst that can enable a bullish price movement. It provides the necessary information needed to identify suitable trades. It also helps when there is a catalyst that encourages a bullish pattern.

Due Diligence

The best and most popular approach to find trades that are used by most swing traders is technical analysis. Your trading platform should have a screener that you can use. If it does not come with one, then you can use a free one such as Finviz. Start by examining technical patterns on a regular basis and preferably at night in order to note the ones that are just about to break out or rebound.

You can also search for stocks that experienced a large upward movement in price direction followed by a brief pullback. In fact, this is what swing traders do most of the time. They try to identify a stock that has had a major rally followed by a pullback.

Spend some time filtering through different stocks and identify a couple that you can swing trade. Once this is done, you will then have to come up with a trading plan. A good trading plan implies that you have determined an appropriate entry point, the most suitable stop loss point, and the best point to collect profits. It is crucial to consolidate your gains at some point, even if the stock continues to gain in price. Should this be the case, then you should consolidate your profits then get back in with a new plan.

Having a good trading plan is crucial for your success. Trading without one is akin to setting yourself up for failure. Therefore, come up with a plan and a reliable risk management strategy. Risk management helps you to manage the exposure of your trading capital so that you limit your losses. Without proper risk management, you could lose most of your trading capital and put a strain on your trading.

How to Trade

Now that you have identified a stock to trade and come up with a trading plan, the next step should be to execute the trade. As soon as you do, you will have to keep yourself updated with the latest happening in the world of finance and perhaps even politics. Watch out for any upcoming events and then weight their strengths in terms of affecting your stock's price movement.

Also, be on the lookout for volatility as this is your friend. A prolonged uptrend is never a good thing. When a stock has an uptrend, you should hope to see a reversal in direction for a brief period of time before the uptrend resumes. This counter-trend provides excellent entry points. It also provides information on potential profit-take points as we as points to exit trades or stop loss points.

You will eventually have to exit your trades. Hopefully, these will have earned you some attractive profits in a short period of time. After exiting your trades, you need to take a pen and a notebook then note down all the things that took place. Write down what steps you took, what worked for you, and possibly what did not work. Put down the reasons that affected your trades and if they were profitable or not.

If you do not write down details of the trade explaining what worked and what didn't, then you are very likely to repeat any mistakes in your next trade. Any lessons learned need to be entered into a journal. This way, you will note all the positives as well as any negatives so as to improve future trades.

The best aspect of swing trading is that you require less energy and less time to trade compared to day trading. It strikes a nice balance between long term trading and day trading. If you are concerned about holding overnight positions, then you need to know that swing trading is one of the most popular and most profitable forms of generating income and profitability.

Investing versus Trading

Trading and investing have numerous similarities. In both instances, an individual or institution uses financial resources to make a profit. However, a closer look at the two shows they are very different from each other. While both a trader and an investor seeking to make a profit from investing in the markets, investors often choose to make huge returns over a prolonged period of time while traders take smaller and frequent profits over a short period of time.

Trading Accounts

Trading accounts include most of all the other accounts discussed previously. These accounts include a lot of small but regular and frequent transactions. The main aim of these accounts is to generate returns that are higher than the long-term or buy-and-hold accounts.

Investors can be happy receiving 10% to 15% return annually, but traders prefer about 10% return each month. Profits on trading accounts normally accrue from buying small amounts at low prices and then selling the same at higher prices. These trades are often carried out in the shortest periods of time.

Trading styles basically refer to the holding time or amount of time between the purchase and sale of securities. Trade accounts, therefore, include day traders, swing traders, position traders, and scalp traders. Scalp traders hold positions in the markets for only a couple of seconds or minutes. There are certain factors that determine the choice of trading style. These include personality, trading experience, and levels of risk tolerance.

Chapter 3: The Trading Mindset

A Look at the Mindset of a Broker

Trading is not all about just profiting from the stock exchange. It involves a lot more. The key to success as a trader is having the right mindset. Traders try out different strategies and develop trading plans so as to perform better after expansive analysis. However, even with these great strategies, they also need to develop winning mindsets.

It is amazing that a lot of great traders incur losses and do not make money at the markets simply because they lack the proper mindset. Many traders believe that the difference between a successful trader and others is the mindset. A trader's psychology is crucial for their success.

Success at the stock market is not about formulating the best strategies or being the smartest or even doing the best market analysis. Once you become a proficient trader, you will then need to develop a winning mindset, which is a good trader's mindset. In fact, it is said that fear is the biggest enemy of any trader.

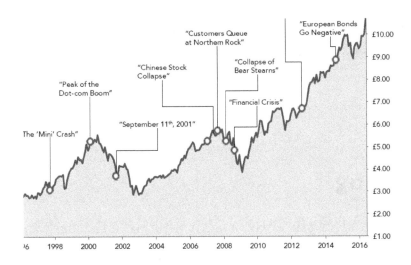

Fear of Losing

One of the biggest drawbacks that are holding back traders and preventing them from winning is fear. They say fear of losing is the greatest obstacle to winning at the markets. Traders fear to enter trades because of fear of losing their trading capital. As such, at the very first sign of trouble, they are ready to exit the markets, take their money and run.

This is all too common, especially with novice traders and beginners. Some traders are of the idea that all it takes is a great trading strategy. They believe that with a great strategy, all they need to do is enter the markets, plug in the great strategy, and start earning top dollar. Unfortunately, the markets don't work this way. Traders with this mentality are setting themselves up not just for failure but also for heartbreak, disappointment, and stress.

Winning

There are traders who are constantly winning in the markets. They consistently make money and are profitable in the short, medium, and long terms. This is possible to achieve but only with the right mindset coupled with successful trading strategies. Therefore, even as you learn how to trade and implement some complex and impressive strategies, you should also learn how to be mentally composed.

The stock market is not about getting rich quickly. Rather, it is more about earning a steady, passive income that can grow quickly over time.

It Is All in the Mind

There is a book written by Norman Welz that is considered the best source of information on the status of a trader's mind. Normal is a trained psychologist who focused on trading psychology. He has extensive experience in this field as he also trades the markets on a regular basis. Apart from writing the book, Norman also spends a lot of his time training traders and helping to direct their minds the right way.

Applied trading psychology is essential for successful trading. When you have the right state of mind coupled with excellent trading strategies, then you can expect to not only see results but maintain great performance on a regular basis at the markets. As it is, traders do need discipline, and this lacks a lot of the time. With discipline, a trader is able to stick to the script and perform as required without deviating from the trading plan.

It is true that trading, just like any other business, is a risky affair, and traders feel the need for added security. In fact, experts are of the opinion that trading is one of the most insecure financial ventures out there. The emotions that it generates are intense and extreme emotions.

The Right Trading Mind

To be a successful trader in the long term and consistently generate a profit, then the right state of mind must be developed. However, we need to realize the fact that lots of our minds have been influenced negatively over the years. There are different ways of influencing the way we think because it has to change.

One of the trusted approaches used by psychologists is training the mind on how to trust. Ideally, most of our actions are based on our subconscious. As such, we tend to repeat mistakes made in the past simply because our brains have been subconsciously trained that way. The good news is that this way of thinking and doing things can be changed.

Behavior Modification

One of the most effective ways of training the mind and introducing positive psychology is to modify a trader's behavior. This modification is undertaken in the correct direction in order to overcome any fear and mental resistance that comes in the way. The process also involves personality modification. When your personality is modified in the correct way, then you should be successful trading. Without this kind of mental training, then you should not really be trading. This is because the emotions that come with trading will get the better of you. You will flounder sooner or later as you implement the different strategies or undertake some of the processes.

The basic purpose of trading psychology is often underestimated. While there is sufficient focus on trading details, including strategies, analysis, and so on, there is often very little attention paid to trading psychology. This is essentially what makes the difference between success and failure in the stock markets.

Focus on Mental Toughness and Stress Management

Trading is a process that revolves mostly around three major factors. These are money management, trading strategies, and psychology. You need to keep in mind that the markets can be a very emotional place, so it is crucial that you remain focused and disciplined. If you do not stay disciplined, then you will lose out, and others will very likely take advantage of you.

What you really need to do in order to trade successfully is to have a solid strategy, follow the strategy, and stick to it. If the strategy does not follow the intended plan, then simply quit and come up with another strategy.

If you have a strong mindset, you will be able to understand when to pursue a losing trade and when to quit. If you lack discipline, then one of two emotions will take over. These are greed and fear.

Sometimes traders trade on a whim and keep posting random trades. Rather than take this approach, you really should focus on a successful strategy which you will pursue until you need to exit. You should also have good trading skills and proper money management plan. With these in place, you will be able to focus better and think in terms of probabilities and risk-reward ratios. This way, you will not leave room for emotional trading.

There are other things that you need to also keep in mind. For instance, you need to develop and stick with good trading habits. As a trader, you need to note that a winner is one who is persistent and consistent. You should develop the habit of closely studying the markets, conducting your analysis, and position sizing.

You also need to accept any possible failures. Sometimes your strategies will not work out, and you will lose some trades. This happens to all traders, even experienced ones. If you assume that you must succeed on each attempt, then you will be setting yourself up for failure.

There are other things that you need to also keep in mind. For instance, you need to develop and stick with good trading habits. As a trader, you need to note that a winner is one who is persistent and consistent. You should develop the habit of closely studying the markets, conducting your analysis, and position sizing.

Position sizing is common, especially in a volatile market. As such, you need to take care of your downside risks and ensure that you position the size appropriately. You should also envision the end game. Come up with a vision of where you want the trade to head then prepare to make any necessary adjustments.

You also need to accept any possible failures. Sometimes your strategies will not work out, and you will lose some trades. This happens to all traders, even experienced ones. If you assume that you must succeed on each attempt, then you will be setting yourself up for failure.

Stoicism and Trading

What is Stoicism?

Stoicism can be defined as a school of ancient Greek Romano philosophy. It was founded by a philosopher and thinker named Zeno of Citium. Stoicism is one of four major schools of philosophy that were prevalent in ancient Greece. There other three are Epicurus' Garden, Aristotle's Lyceum, and Plato's Academy.

The Stoic philosophy teaches us how to live a fulfilling life without all the unnecessary stress, depression, anxiety, worry, and all other negative issues. The teachings focus on four main ideas in their teachings. These are control, nature, emotions, and value.

According to the stoics, there are only very few things that we have control over. These include decisions that we make and the actions that we take. Most things that occur to us are often beyond our control. As such, we tend to be unhappy, stressed out, angry, and so on due to factors that are beyond our control. This is the major mistake that most people make and hence the source of their unhappiness. We need to focus on the few things that we have control over. Only then will we be able to find happiness and tranquility.

When it comes to emotions, we often encounter two main types, mostly. These are emotions of happiness and also those of anger and dejection. Many times, we tend to make mistakes and suffer the consequences. Life is difficult and challenging, and most people accept that. Instead of letting these issues bother us, we should focus on the things that we can change. When we harbor harmful thoughts and emotions based on flawed thinking and emotions, then we really solve nothing at all.

According to stoicism principles, we humans thrive when we accept the things that occur to us. As human beings, we should not allow ourselves to be disillusioned by our fear of suffering and pair or controlled by our desires for wealth and pleasure. This is possible through understanding that our powers are limited. We are only able to control a number of things in our lives. The rest of the things that occur to us are beyond our control.

It is advisable, therefore, to understand the way the world works and to play our part as far as nature is concerned. It is crucial that we focus on understanding the way that the world works and to play each one a part in nature. Stoicism also supports just and fair treatment of every person and working together in harmony.

Develop a Morning Routine

You need to have a defined morning routine. The first step as soon as you wake up is to prepare yourself mentally for the tasks ahead. The world is a tough place. We can expect to meet horrible and unreasonable people in the course of the day. Many are probably liars, busybodies, jealous, and so on. Understanding that the world is full of evil people is crucial. This way, you will be prepared whenever things get out of hand.

You should also spend some time reflecting on the coming day. Always look on the inside and examine yourself. Think about the previous day and the things that you managed to overcome. Did you encounter any challenges? How did you respond to situations? Do these things the minute you wake up and sometimes do it before sleeping.

Always Be Time Conscious

We need to always keep in mind that we have very limited time on this earth. Yet our time is quite limited. With each passing day, our mind ages, our skin dies, our relationships fizzle out, and our bodies breakdown. Time is always in motion, and with each tick of the clock, we lose precious moments that will never be recovered.

If you pay close attention to each day, you will realize that we have a tendency to postpone matters that are of utmost importance to us. We need to learn from Marcus Aurelius. Each night he spent some time decompressing. He wrote down the events of the day, reviewed it, and thought of how to perform better next time. Learn how to prioritize the most important things and then accomplish these first. Then proceed to accomplish all other things in order of importance. This way, you will have conquered procrastination.

Spend some time each day thinking about the things you have to do and accomplish. As a trader, you have to come up with a trading plan that will include lots of things, such as developing a trading strategy. You will need to determine which trades to enter, which stocks to choose, and amounts to allocate to each trade. It is imperative that you pause and think about these things, as you will be able to critically analyze each step.

Think about the bad or negative things that could happen and then start thinking about all the positives. Focus on how you want things to work out for you. What steps can lead to a positive outcome? Think about these steps and focus on them. If your focus is on the positive and you follow this up with action, then you will stand a much better chance of success than focusing only on trade. A lot of traders and even experts believe trading is all a matter of instituting strategies and has nothing to do with mental toughness.

This is really wrong and misadvised. Trade practices have a huge mental impact on traders. So many traders are confused, worried, and concerned, especially at the prospect of losing money and losing out on different trades. At the first sign of loss, some traders tend to run. They withdraw their funds and cancel trades. This is so wrong because the markets travel in both directions.

Some strategies may go wrong, even with the best planning. As such, traders should not despair. Stoicism teaches us to understand that any situation is not even close to being the worst situation possible. Compare losing some money trading with getting an incurable disease such as cancer. It could be worse, such as contracting a serious viral disease, dying in a plane crash, or even drowning in the sea.

Choose Not to Be Harmed

According to the Stoics, there is no bad or good but only perception. This means that all things happening to us are neither good nor bad. All that is simply a matter of perception, and that is within our control. As such, we should take charge and control perception.

If your initial perception of loss was that it is a bad thing, then you can always go back and change your thinking to view every aspect of trading in a positive manner. You can think of any losses you make as a learning experience and a great opportunity to better your trading skills. Therefore, you will no longer fear trading or even fear losing. Instead, you will have an all-round experience where winning is viewed positively, and losing is also viewed positively.

Also, remember that stoics spend a lot of their time focusing on their lives and how they can do better in everything they do and how they can be useful to those around them. This means being happier and addressing any issues that you may be facing.

Challenges viewed from this aspect cease to be daunting and remain positive endeavors worth tackling.

Brief Outline of a Trader's Mindset

As a trader, you need to learn how to execute trades at the stock markets for maximum profits. You also need to have the right mindset because learning how to trade only is insufficient. Therefore, always remember that people trade to make money, but some trades can lose you money.

You will not win all your trades. All traders, even the best and most experienced of them all win some and lose some. The only difference is how you treat your losses or how you view them. If you think of them as learning experiences and not the worst thing in the world, then you will have developed a positive mindset.

However, if you are scared of trading or losing money, then you should not trade because you will lose money. You need to first work on your mental focus and mindset before embarking on the markets or the trading process. Once your mind is focused, you should always trade with confidence and not worry about the outcome.

Procedure for Trading with the Right Mindset

First, you will need to ensure that your trading skills are up to scratch. If they are not, then you will need to keep practicing and learning. Once you are confident enough about all aspects of trading, such as choosing the right stocks, finding the trend, strategy, and so on, then you should come up with a trading plan.

A good trading plan takes care of all aspects of the trade. You will first come up with a strategy and then write it down. Check it out thoroughly so that you eliminate any errors. Once you have a foolproof strategy, come up with a complete trading plan. This means determining the stocks to buy when to enter the markets, exit points, when to collect profits, the strategy to apply and so on. You should also determine the amounts to allocate to each trade.

Once you have a sure plan, the next step would be to implement it as planned. This is the best approach to trading. All too often, traders change their minds and start adjusting their plans based on market conditions. This is totally wrong and is what trading psychology is all about. If you have a sure plan, you should implement it without any changes or major alterations. This is the only way to emerge as the winner in any trading situation.

If you follow this approach and implement your trading plan without alterations or hesitations, you will emerge the winner most of the time. Sometimes traders lose focus. Even after practicing and learning to trade for numerous years, they still are not able to return a profit because their minds are not properly aligned.

Trading plans are supposed to be accurate, back-tested, and foolproof. This means that you should ensure that you go through each and every step before implementation. As such, there should be no hesitation on the trading platform. Simply follow your trading plan through then note any mistakes and write them down in a trading journal.

Trading Psychology Tips

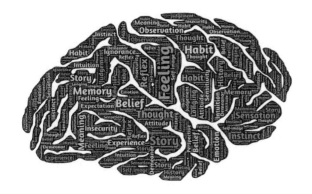

There are other things that you need to also keep in mind. For instance, you need to develop and stick with good trading habits. As a trader, you need to note that a winner is one who is persistent and consistent. You should develop the habit of closely studying the markets, conducting your analysis, and position sizing.

Position sizing is rather common, especially in a volatile market. As such, you need to take care of your downside risks and ensure that your position size appropriately. You should also envision the end game. Come up with a vision of where you want the trade to head then prepare to make any necessary adjustments.

You also need to accept any possible failures. Sometimes your strategies will not work out, and you will lose some trades. This happens to all traders, even experienced ones. If you assume that you must succeed on each attempt, then you will be setting yourself up for failure.

What you really need to do in order to trade successfully is to have a solid strategy, follow the strategy, and stick to it. If the strategy does not follow the intended plan, then simply quit and come up with another strategy.

If you have a strong mindset, you will be able to understand when to pursue a losing trade and when to quit. If you lack discipline, then one of two emotions will take over. These are greed and fear.

Sometimes traders trade on a whim and keep posting random trades. Rather than take this approach, you really should focus on a successful strategy which you will pursue until you need to exit. You should also have excellent trading skills and proper money management plan. With these in place, you will be able to focus better and think in terms of probabilities and risk-reward ratios. This way, you will not leave room for emotional trading.

Additional Trading Tips

Remember That The Trend Is Your Friend

You need to keep in mind that the trend of the underlying security always works in your favor. Once you identify the trend based on your chart analysis, you should then identify the trend and follow it. If you go with the trend, then you are very likely going to succeed.

On the other hand, going against the trend is a dangerous and risky venture. It is highly advisable to go with the trend and never against it. Resistance is futile, while momentum is actually your friend.

Keep a Look Out for Earnings Release

It is absolutely crucial when trading stocks and options that you should be on the lookout for earnings release dates and announcements. These announcements have a huge impact on markets, stock prices, and options.

There is usually an anticipation of earnings reports because strong or weak earnings could cause the value of the underlying stock to move in either direction significantly.

What happens is that options prices will decline shortly after an earnings release announcement. Once the earnings report is over, and the market receives the information, stock prices will basically resume normal levels. The volatility will eventually subside.

Ride on a Winner If You Come Across One

Stock market experts often advise traders to "ride your winners." This simply means that if you get a profitable trade, then you should stick with it for as long as you can. It is advisable to let the stock price continue with its movement for as long as it is profitable.

Inexperienced traders may wish to cash out then get back in. However, experienced traders will stick with a trade and ride it to the end. Momentum is likely to carry it further.

Learn to Cut Your Losses

Novice traders often stick to a trade even when it is losing money. They often believe that they can recoup the losses. However, sometimes, you need to admit that your strategy did not work out, cut your losses, and exit a trade. It is a fact that all traders lose out on some trades and win others. The difference is the number of those lost versus wins or perhaps the amounts made versus amounts lost.

In brief, knowing how to trade only is insufficient. You need to have the right mentality or mental attitude in order to trade profitably at the bourse. This has been determined by the experts, so learn these good trading psychology tips, and you will be successful in your trading ventures over the months and years.

Chapter 4: The Best Stocks for Swing Trading

If you wish to identify the best stocks for swing trading, then you need to understand fundamental trading. Remember that fundamental analysis is the close scrutiny and inspections of companies' management, strategy, performance, history, and future. Most fundamentalists are also swing traders because company fundamentals take a long time to change.

Price movements take quite a while before making any significant movements. This is why fundamental traders are swing traders. Swing trading often takes a couple of days to even weeks and months before a trade moves into positive territory.

Making Important Determinations

As a trader, you need to take a number of factors into consideration when deciding which stocks to trade. Swing trading lies somewhere between trend trading and day trading. Day traders hold onto stocks or market positions for only a couple of hours while trend traders hold onto them for months or weeks.

There are certain factors that determine the kind of stocks that you trade. These include the amount of capital accessible to you, your level of experience, and the type of style, though, in this case, we are looking at swing trading. The criteria selected should actually constitute part of the plan of selecting stocks. Also, it should constitute part of your trading plan.

Trading plans need to be dynamic. This is because as you grow and gain more experience as a trader, you will learn a few crucial factors, gain more knowledge and more insights, and hence make adjustments accordingly. Here are a couple of points to consider as you choose stocks for trading.

Points to Ponder on Picking Suitable Stocks

First, you need to come to terms with your own levels of risk and then determine the most appropriate level. Different traders have different levels and appetites. Always consider this first.

It is also advisable to think of ways of identifying stocks that are most suitable for trade purposes. For instance, you can decide to trade in Blue-chip stocks with large volumes and excellent performance over the years. Others may have different approaches, but this is just one.

Also, choose one stock first and then analyze its results before moving onto the next one. This approach is more effective than randomly or generally identifying stocks.
Make use of trading charts and other tools available to you. This is an effective and reliable approach because tools are a lot more accurate compared to others. Charts will reveal information about the stock movement and the markets overall trend.

Once you come up with a trading plan, you should ensure that you stick with it. Do not change things midway as this can have profound effects later. It has been proven time and time again that traders who stick to their trading plans are successful, while those who fail to do so aren't as successful.

Screening Stocks for Trading

There are a few basic steps that you can follow in order to identify ideal trading stocks. You first need to come up with a general list of stocks that you wish to investigate further. These are stocks that qualify through the basic screening process and happen to be in industries that you understand. Once you have this basic list, you may then proceed to do more in-depth research and analysis to actually identify the kind of stock you are looking for. You can search for shares that you like through databases such as SEDAR for Canadian firms and EDGAR for US-based companies.

There are tons of free web-based tools that can assist you in searching and screening for stocks and shares. Think of tools such as Yahoo stock Screener or Google Stock Screener. These are free and readily accessible. You can get even more details results by using paying sites such as Y-Chart Stock Screener. Screeners generally analyze thousands of stocks and then screen them according to the criteria that you provide. One of the most important search criteria used is P/E. You can set the screeners to only find stocks with P/E lower than 15. Screeners will do just that and only show you companies with P/E lower than 15.

Consider Your Personality

There is a variety of things that need to be considered when choosing stocks for trading purposes. One of these is your personality. People have different personalities, and these are in many ways, shaped by our experiences and environments.

If you grew up loving fast cars and enjoy tinkering with technology, then you may want to consider stocks in the field of technology. If you love math and are in the finance or banking sector, then stocks in the field of finance would be ideal for your case. This is because you have a deeper and more intimate understanding of the happenings in this world than other people.

Some people love sports, while others enjoy watching movies. Whatever your preferences and personality, there is always a sector that will work just fine for you. If you spend most of your career in the shipping and transport sectors, then consider stocks in related fields. This way, you will understand the happenings in these sectors and will have better intuition and understanding when there are reports, financial audits, or major news announcements.

Some things can be pointless. For instance, someone in the world of finance may not understand much about mining. Therefore, buying stocks in this field may not be a great idea. The same is true about a trader in the field of transport choosing stocks in the field of mining or manufacturing.

How to Identify Undervalued Stocks

There are some stocks in the market that are undervalued and others that could be overvalued. Many investors and traders are always on the lookout for undervalued stocks to add to their portfolios. A lot of investors are of the view that identifying undervalued stocks is one way of finding great investments. This is because these stocks are often priced at levels far below their underlying values. To understand this concept of value investing, we need to understand a couple of things.

Understand Why Some Securities Are Undervalued

It is important that you understand as much as possible about value investing. Therefore, you need to learn and understand why some stocks or securities become undervalued. One of the crucial reasons for value investing is because of stock markets sometimes under prices stocks occasionally. There are reasons why this happens, so let us look at some of these reasons.

Market corrections and crashes: When the market drops, then investors are provided with an excellent chance to search for a variety of undervalued stocks.

Cyclic fluctuations: These tend to happen from time to time where some sectors outperform others. This happens at various stages of the regular economic cycle. The sectors that are disadvantaged by the fluctuations often offer excellent sources for undervalued stocks.

Bad news: Whenever there is bad news, it results in serious knee-jerk reactions that cause stock prices to plummet far more than they should. This is almost similar to stocks, not meeting analyst's expectations.

Missed expectations: In some instances, quarterly results can fall far short of expectation. This can be a pretty serious issue and can cause shares to plunge a lot more than they should.

Now, if you wish to screen for undervalued stocks and shares, then you should confine your efforts only to businesses that you understand. However, this only applies to investors. Apparently, far too many investors venture into industries that they do not wholly understand, and this puts their investments at risk.

You also need to understand the related terminology and metrics essential for stock evaluation. While there are tons of metrics, only a few are crucial, and you should learn.

Important Related Terminology

There are plenty of metrics related to stock evaluation. For our purposes, we only need to learn some of them and not all. Here are some metrics that are essential for identifying undervalued stocks.

P/E or Price to Earnings Ratio: One of the most useful metrics used to evaluate stocks is P/E or price to earnings ratio. This ratio is obtained simply by dividing the current stock price with its annual earning. The result will give a metric that can be used to compare firms within the same industry or sector. Ideally, a lower P/E ratio means the stock is undervalued. However, this is just one among many other metrics.

Price-to-Earnings to Growth or PEG: This is another important ratio used to determine undervalued stocks. You calculate the PEG by dividing the P/E ratio with the projected earnings growth rate within a given period of time. It is crucial to also use this value to compare the performance of a business vis-à-vis the performance of other firms in the same sector.

Return on Equity or ROE: A return on equity is yet another metric you can use to find undervalued stocks. ROE stands for a firm's annual net income calculated as a percentage of shareholders' equity. In short, this metric measures the efficiency of a company in investing funds to create wealth.

Debt to Equity Ratio: the debt to equity ratio is a ratio that is arrived at by working out a firm's total debt and dividing this debt with total shareholders' equity.

Current Ratio: The current ratio is more of a liquidity related metric. It is arrived at by taking a company's current assets and dividing it by the total of its current liabilities. This ratio informs investors of the ease at which a firm is able to repay its short-term debt.

You should begin evaluating stocks in order to get a feel for some of these metrics. You can also develop your very own evaluation criteria to enable you to find undervalued stocks in the market.

Volatility

As a trader, you want to find stocks with sufficient market activity. This means identifying volatile stocks. Stocks that are volatile generally move up and down a lot. They will trend upward one time then fall the next moment and even spike in either direction. Such stocks are a trader's best friend. This is because traders profit from volatility

Volatility is always measured using a variable known as Beta. You need to learn and understand how beta works so that you can apply it to stocks that you wish to trade.

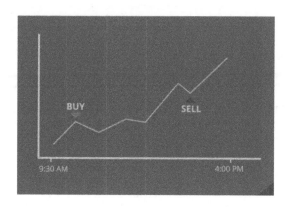

What is Beta?

Beta is defined as the measure of the volatility of a stock or any other security. The beta of a stock is simply the volatility of the stock in relation to the entire market. The market is thought to have a beta of 1.0. All other stocks are measured in relation to their deviation from the entire market. The deviation, in this case, refers to the volatility of a stock.

Beta is a product of the CAPM or capital asset pricing model and is generally used to measure the volatility or risk profile of security. A stock that moves or deviates by values less than that of the market will have a beta value of less than 1.0. On the other hand, a stock that deviates by values greater than those of the market will have beta values greater than 1.0.

The capital asset pricing model, or CAPM, works out the possible return of financial security using both expected market returns and beta. Beta, in terms of statistics, is akin to the slope that traverses across numerous data points from the returns of security versus data points of the market.

CAPM or capital asset pricing model is generally relied on to determine the cost of equity. Generally, the higher the beta value is the more will be the value of the capital discount rate. In summary, we can conclude that beta has a major effect on a company's stock valuation.

How to Calculate Beta

Beta represents the activities of a stock's return relative to volatility or swings prevalent in the market. The best way to work out beta is by regression analysis. Beta indicates the likelihood of stock to react to swings and volatility in the market. There is a standard formula used to determine the value of beta.

This formula for determining the value of beta is basically the covariance of the income received from stocks with the income due to a benchmark dividend divided by the variation of the income of the benchmark dividend.

Beta = Covariance (Re, Rm) / **Variance** (Rm)

Re stands for returns based on a stock
Rm stands for the overall market's returns

Variance refers to the extent of the market's data spread from the mean value
Covariance is the change in a security's returns in relation to the changes seen in the returns of the market.

Risk Management is a Crucial Consideration

Another crucial factor that comes to play when selecting stocks is risk management. Different traders have varying appetites for risks. More experienced traders who enter complex or advanced positions can afford great risks. As a novice trader, you should opt for lower-risk strategies and take as little risk with your funds as possible.

Also, think about investing not more than ten percent of your trading capital per trade. Therefore, if you have about $10,000 as your capital, do not allocate more than $100 for each trade. This way, you will be minimizing your risk and reducing exposure.

More on Risk Management

Risk management is a term that refers to the process of managing any possible and potential risks. Risks are possible and can occur at any time. They are inherent, and as such, traders need to take the necessary precautions to avoid losing money. As such, you need to learn about risk management if you are to be successful as a swing trader.

Risk management is an essential approach to investing as the trader greatly reduces any potential for losses. If the trader had invested the fund in securities such as stock options or futures, then the investment would have been highly risky. Risk management takes place almost all the time like when an investor or fund manager or investor analyses risk and decides to make adjustments in order to minimize or prevent any inherent risks.

Risk management could be as simple as purchasing one security instead of another, or it could be a rather complex process. Think about traders who venture into complex securities such as futures and derivatives. Such instruments require serious risk management techniques as these complex securities are highly

98

risky even though they are also highly rewarding when successful.

Basically, risk management happens when traders endeavor to measure potential losses and then take specific action to take mitigating action against the risks. This will also depend on their appetite for risk. New and novice traders should avoid risky ventures and should only pursue ventures that are within their risk appetite.

Risk Management Intrigues

It is extremely crucial that every trader considers risk management in order to avert possible losses in their trades. Without risk management, then traders and investors would just as well resort to gambling. Risk assessment and management ensure sufficient steps are taken to prevent losses.

There are great examples in the recent history of poor risk management approach that led to hundreds of billions in losses incurred by investors. Here we are talking about the collapse of the housing sector in 2007 / 2008 in the United States. Apparently, plenty of homeowners and mortgage holders across the country lost their investments due to the subprime mortgage collapse.

This collapse led to the great recession that followed thereafter. It took the US a couple of years to recover from this catastrophe, which also affected other sectors. The entire problem was a result of investments without proper risk management solutions.

Back then, anyone who wanted a house was sold one even when they could not afford it. Homebuyers took out mortgage loans and bought homes that were way out of their reach. These mortgages were then packaged into a form of security (MBS or Mortgage-Backed Securities) and sold off at the securities markets. The resulting fallout was extremely large, with the collapse of major banks such as Lehman Brothers.

Risk is Not Necessarily a Negative Thing

People mostly tend to think of risk as a bad thing. They view it negatively and think of ways of shunning it. Risk does not have to be viewed in negative or derogatory terms. It actually is a good thing and can save investors and traders from losing their resources.

Numerous investors tend to define investment risk simply as a deviation or variation from an expected result. However, some of the most successful traders engage in very risky investments. The payoff is that they take the time to weigh the risks and even take measures to protect their investments.

Good examples are options and futures traders. Options and futures are considered high risk yet high reward investments. If these investments and trading strategies were extremely risky, then nobody would touch them. However, there are those who focus solely on these highly risky ventures, yet they are the most successful and very profitable. It all basically comes down to proper risk management techniques. As an advanced trader, you need to be able to implement appropriate risk management techniques so that your trades are safe and secure.

One crucial factor that traders need to keep in mind is their appetite for risk. How much risk is one able to take? There is always a risk when venturing into the financial markets. However, an investor's appetite for risk will determine his or her strategy as well as the relevant risk-mitigating measures. This way, it will be possible to invest securely with little worry should things not work out as desired.

Tips and Advice

Start by Planning Your Trades

The single most crucial aspect of your trade should be risk management. Without it, your whole trading life will be in jeopardy. Therefore, start all your trading ventures with a plan that you intend to stick by. Traders have a saying that you should plan your trades and then trade your plan. This means to come up with the best plan possible and then implement it and stick by it. Trade is very similar to war. When it is well planned, it can be won before it is executed.

Some of the best tools you will need as part of your risk management plan are take-profit and stop-loss. Using these two tools, you can plan your trades in advance. You will need to use technical analysis in order to determine these two points. With this information, you should be able to determine the price you are willing to pay as well as the losses you can incur.

Always Observe the One Percent Rule

Traders often apply what is known as the one percent rule. This rule dictates that you should not risk amounts greater than one percent of your total trading capital on one single trade. For instance, if you have $15,000 as your trading capital, then you should never risk more than $150 on a single trade. This is a great risk management approach that you can use as part of your trading strategy. Most traders who adopt this strategy usually have amounts less than $100,000 in their trading accounts. There are some who are so more confident, so they choose to work with 2% instead.

Ensure That You Set Target and Stops

We can define a stop-loss as the total amount of loss that a trader is willing to incur in a single trade. Beyond the stop-loss point, the trader exits the trade. This is basically meant to prevent further losses by thinking the trade will eventually get some momentum. We also have what is known as a take-profit point. It is at this point that you will collect any profits made and possibly exit a trade. At this point, stock or other security is often very close to the point of resistance.

Beyond this point, a reversal in price is likely to take place. Rather than lose money, you should exit the trade. Traders sometimes take profit and let trade continue if it was still making money. Another take-profit point is then plotted. If you have a good run, you are allowed to lock in the profits and let the good run continue.

Use Indicators Such as Moving Averages

The best way to identify these two crucial points is to use moving averages. The reason why we prefer moving averages to determine the stop-loss and take-profit points. These are closely tracked by the markets and very simple to determine. Some of the popular moving averages include the 5-day, 20-day, 50-day, 100-day, and 200-day averages. Simply apply these to your security's chart then make a determination about the best points.

You can also use support and resistance lines to determine the take-profit and stop-loss points. This is also a pretty simple process. Simply connect past lows and highs that happened in the recent past on key, high-than-normal volume levels. They work on the same principle as the moving averages. All that you need to do is to find levels where the price action will respond to the trend line on areas of high volume.

Bull Versus Bear Markets

The terms bull market and bear market are commonly used by traders and investors and throughout the financial world. Not all who use these terms or hear them understand exactly what they mean. Yet they are crucial and affect our trading strategies and plans. As a trader, you can expect to hear these two terms used a lot, and it is important that you understand what they mean as well as the crucial similarities and differences.

Bull Markets

A bull market is a market that trends upwards for a given period of time. The markets are mostly on such a trend most of the time. The trend may start after a period of decline, followed by stability. An upward trend in the market means that stock prices are on the rise, the economy is doing well, and the outlook is generally positive. As such, more and more traders and investors seek to invest their money during this period.

There are a number of factors that result in a bull market. These are low-interest rates, a booming or strong economy, high employment rates, and great government policies that support growth. Under such circumstances, the bull market will enjoy a long run, and both traders and investors will thrive.

Bear Markets

A bear market is the exact opposite of a bull market. The market trends downwards, and stock prices fall. An observer would say that the market movement is moving in a downward direction quarter after quarter. When quantified, a bear market loses ground by about twenty percent. This means the trend tends negatively with a 20% loss each quarter.

There are certain factors that cause bear markets. One of these is a lack of employment, and another is a poorly performing economy. A successful economy is one where employment rates are high, and interest rates are low. On the other hand, a poorly performing economy is one where interest rates are high, there are fewer than desired jobs, and government policies are unfriendly towards businesses.

Bear markets cause a lot of worry and concern in a lot of people, especially traders and investors. Many take out their investments from the markets from fear of losing out. As such, depression tends to set in, and the economy starts to underperform.

There are reasons why the terms bull market and bear market are used. A bull attacks by striking upwards hence the term bull for a market that's headed upwards. A bear attacks by swiping downwards towards its victim during an attack. This is why the term bear market is used. The markets tend to experience bull runs most of the time, which are followed by brief bear markets less than 30 percent of the time.

Chapter 5: Platforms for Swing Trading

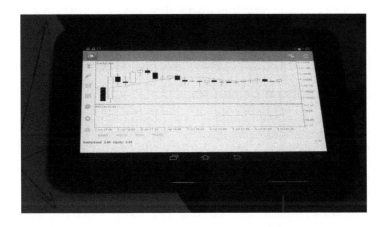

Swing trading action takes place on trading platforms provided by brokers. As a swing trader, once you perfect your skills, you will need to identify a suitable platform to apply your skills. Brokers happen to be the best providers of trading platforms, as they are also connected directly to the markets. If you wish to trade live, then you had better source your trading platform from a renowned broker.

Essentials of a Suitable Trading Platform

A good trading platform is one that enables users, especially traders, access to all the tools and software necessary for successfully executing trades. This means tools to perform stock searches for fundamental analysis, technical analysis, making comparisons, and so much more.

Sometimes it takes a while to identify the best trading platform. This is where brokers come in handy. Numerous brokers take time to market themselves and their services on the internet. This is great because traders are made aware of the facilities and brokerage firms available. However, it is much better to find recommendations and look for references before signing up with a broker. Marketing can be easy, but recommendations carry more weight and are generally more reliable.

Further Details of Trading Platforms

Trading platforms are programs or software that is designed for trading purposes. They are specifically designed to accomplish a number of tasks, including opening and entering market positions, closing, and also managing these different positions.

These activities are normally achieved via brokers who have direct access to the trading floor.

Brokers offer access to these platforms either for free or at a price. As a trader, you will need to log into your broker account, fund it, and then begin trading on the provided platform. Some of these platforms are pretty basic, while others feature the latest tools and modern applications.

Summary

Trading platforms are essentially software programs and tools that are used by traders and investors to execute trades and manage positions at the stock markets.

There is a wide variety of platforms available. They range from the most basic to the more sophisticated and complex platforms that can execute numerous trades and manage them prudently.

Most of these software programs come with useful tools, a variety of screens, features, and programs that can accomplish a number of useful feats. For instance, a trader using a trading platform can receive direct feeds from the trading floor, can search databases for information, and even

There are various factors that should be taken into account when choosing the most appropriate platforms. Cost is one of the factors, but others include ease of use, customer support, features included and so on. Other factors that should be considered include balance and account trade-offs.

Features of a Trading Platform

Most trading platforms come bundled up, complete with other additional features. These are charting tools, real-time quotes, market access tools, trading news sources, financial calculators, and much more.

Some platforms are dedicated to trading stocks only, or options only, and perhaps currency only. Others are more flexible and can handle a myriad of securities such as stocks, indexes, currencies, options, and so on.

There are two basic kinds of trading platforms. These are commercial platforms and pro platforms. Commercial platforms are for the average retail trader like you and I. They come with a number of useful features such as charts and news feeds and all other things you need for detailed research as well as investor education.

The prop platforms are customized by designers to suit the needs of professional traders and big corporate brokers or firms. Such firms have specific needs and requirements which can be tailored by software designers and computer programmers.

Brokers

A broker is an individual or firm with direct access to the stock markets. Brokers enable members of the public to trade at the stock market via their platforms. Therefore, if you wish to trade and invest in the stock market, you would most likely need to contact a broker. Fortunately, you do not need to visit their offices because all this is possible online.

Simply identify a suitable broker, open an account, provide basic information, answer a couple of questions, and then begin trading as soon as possible. You will need to fund your account prior to buying stocks. Therefore, find out the different funding options available and determine the amount you wish to deposit. Brokers often have certain requirements such as a minimum deposit amount, and so on. Make sure you are aware of this in order to remain compliant.

Now, you cannot simply visit a stock exchange and purchase stocks. Your online broker will assist you with this. The broker can also advise you on what stocks to buy and so on. You can buy stocks and hold as you wait for the price to go up and then sell to make a profit. This is a very viable option, and a lot of retail traders do this on an ongoing basis. Alternatively, you can choose to buy stocks and hold them for as long as possible, possibly even for years.

Choosing a Trading Platform

There are factors that different traders take into consideration when choosing a trading platform. One of these is the fees charged on that platform. Traders need to balance the need to reduce costs with the desire to have access to a wide variety of crucial tools, resources, and applications.

Swing traders and others such as day traders need to look out for platforms charging low and affordable fees. Keeping costs is crucial because small amounts do add up pretty fast. As such, it is advisable to identify platforms that charge low amounts in order to capitalize on opportunities. Some platforms gobble up traders' profits leaving them with meager earnings. It is advisable to avoid these and turn towards affordable platforms.

Also important are the features that are provided. As a swing trader, you will need access to a number of features that should be provided on the trading platform. As you check out these profiles, try and identify those with features that are desirable. You may want to balance the need for lower fees and charges with the need for quality and crucial features.

Another factor to consider is whether platforms are independent or are only able to function with certain brokers or intermediaries. This happens most of the time, and insiders in the trading field endeavor to lock in their customers to certain brokerage firms and their intermediaries. If they have a good reputation with lots of features and low fees, then they may be considered.

Finally, remember that each platform will require a certain minimum amount for any trader wishing to open an account. Some require a deposit of about $25,000, while others require lesser or even larger amounts. Always check all these features and requirements prior to signing up.

In short, you should have access to a platform that covers all the different situations that you might expect to encounter. A good platform is one that protects your profits with a variety of risk management tools.

Swing traders need to be able to react swiftly to different market conditions and a variety of situations. The right tools and software will enable you to react on time and benefit on price movements or enter trades at the right moments.

Platforms for Swing Traders

There is a variety of platforms available to swing traders. They come with a number of different features. These include premium research functions, news feed, charting tools, and even real-time price quotes. These additional features and tools enhance a trader's performance and make it easier to execute trades faster and accurately. Most platforms available today are designed for different financial instruments like Forex, stocks, futures, and options.

We basically have two different types of platforms. These are commercial platforms and prop platforms. Commercial platforms are mostly used by traders such as swing traders, retail investors, and day traders. They are largely easy to use and come with a myriad of features such as charts and a news feed.

As a swing trader, you will most likely be using commercial platforms provided by different brokerage firms. Even then, there are some things that you need to be on the lookout before choosing one. For instance, what are the included features? How about costs and fees charged? Also, different traders will require different tools on their platforms. There are certain tools that are suitable for day and swing traders, while others are more suitable for options and futures traders.

Examples of Swing Trading Platforms

The Home Trading System

The home trading system is an algorithm and trading software designed to improve performance. Using this system, you can expect to make smarter, faster, and better trading decisions. This particular platform comes with innovative features and a custom algorithm that combines seamlessly to provide a real-time fully integrated trading platform. You are bound to benefit from this platform and experience the benefits of seamless trading complete with all the features that you need.

The platform is completely compatible with some of the most dynamic and highly reliable charting tool. It is able to work with all kinds of markets, from stocks to Forex and indices. The platform is compatible with a variety of bars, such as range and momentum bars, as well as tick charts.

The designers of this platform took great care to consider all the different kinds of traders. This is why this specific platform is suitable for day traders, swing traders, Forex traders, retail investors, and long-term traders. The Home Trading System constitutes a modular platform that consists of different core features. A lot of these features can easily be switched off and on depending on the situation or to suit a particular requirement.

One of the advantages of this platform is that it endeavors to make trading extremely simple. For instance, the algorithm automatically colors the candlesticks or bars a red or blue color in order to provide a clear view of the market conditions and trends. The system will continue following the trends and mark any major changes in a contrasting color. For instance, whenever there is a trigger bar, these will appear in a different color so that it is clear to you the trader that there is definite variation in the trend.

This color feature not only makes trading easy but also improves your trading psychology so that you can trade with very little worry. Other desirable parameters that are essential to your trades are also provided on the platform. For instance, you need accurate and reliable trading signals delivered at the right time. Fortunately, the Home Trading System is designed to provide these signals in a timely and accurate manner.

When there is a turning point in the momentum of stock in the markets, then this will be detected, and a change of color will clearly indicate the turning point. You will be able to see a blue color with contrasting orange color pointing out areas of interest. The dots will indicate the entry points, exit points, collect profit points and so on. A stopping point is also indicated just in case the trade does not work out as planned and you need to exit.

The Entry Zone Platform

We also have a swing trading platform known as the Entry Zone. This platform has been around for a while but has recently undergone a complete overhaul. It has received a new design to specifically address the needs of swing traders. There is no trader in the entire world who wants to join an over-extended market even when it features a large stop-loss point.

One of the main benefits of this specific platform is that it helps eliminate the challenge of entering an overly extended market. It starts by first checking for a pullback. It does this by accessing the 60-minute timeframe. This way, you will be protected from accessing the markets at the worst moment. The algorithm is able to proceed and track the markets so that you eventually get to find out the best market entry points.

Able Trend Trading Platform

This is another platform designed with swing traders in mind. One of its most outstanding features is its ability to instantly identify changes in the trend. Trend direction is first indicated by a distinct color. When the signal is headed upwards, then the color is blue, and when it heads downwards, it changes color to red. If there is any sideways movement then the color changes once more to green.

This platform, therefore, makes it pretty easy to observe the market trend and keep abreast of it. Additional information will then enable you to make the necessary trade moves that you need to as a swing trader. For instance, you will notice red and blue dots on your screen. These indicate the various stop points. When there is a downward trend, then the red dots will indicate your sell points while blue dots will indicate your buy points on the upward trend. These stop points ensure that you partake of the large market movements but with very little risk or exposure.

The reason why this system is so successful is that it comes with state-of-the-art features. It generates dot and bars colors that you can choose for the different bar charts. These include the 5 minutes, 1 minute, daily, tick, and weekly charts. Many traders have termed this platform as both robust and functional. It is a universal platform that can work with different trading systems.

You are able to make large profits if you are able to enter the markets and join the trend at an early stage. Identifying the trend is easy when you have this software. Remember that the trend is a friend of any swing trader. Therefore, spend some time at the beginning of your trades to identify the trend and then move on from here. Identifying the trend at an early stage is what you wish to do. The risks to you are minimal at this stage. This platform helps you identify the trend and provide you with additional crucial information that even large investors do not have.

You are able to operate on any market so that you are not limited to trading stocks only. If you wish to swing trade options, currencies, and other instruments, then you are free to do so. The platform is suitable for all trading styles, including day trading, swing trading, and position trading, and so on.

Interactive Brokers

This is a popular platform that has been recently revamped. It is a highly rated software because of the useful tools available to traders. Some of these tools are extremely useful to sophisticate or seasoned traders who need more than just the basics.

This platform is able to connect you to any and all exchanges across the world. For instance, you may want to trade markets in Hong Kong, Australia, and so on. The software is able to seamlessly connect so that you have great trading experience.

This platform has seen the addition of new features that make trading even easier. These are, however, more suitable to seasoned traders who are more sophisticated than the average retail investor or small trader.

One of the attractive features of Interactive Brokers is that it is a very affordable platform to use. It is especially cost-friendly to small scale traders, retail investors, and the ordinary swing trader as the margin rates are low and affordable.

The platform supports trading across 120 markets located in at least 31 countries and deals in more than 23 different currencies. It also supports traders who execute trades pretty fast.

Additional Considerations

The strategy is also crucial. As a swing trader, your strategy is to buy and hold for a couple of days or weeks. There are crucial factors that you need to consider even as you choose a trading platform. For instance, how much automation do you require? Are there any manual functions that are necessary? How about risk management? What kinds of management approaches do you desire to cut losses and lock profits? A good level of functionality is definitely necessary.

There is also the issue of cost that you have to consider. As a trader, you can expect to incur some costs. Generally, if you are a regular swing trader trading in stocks, then regular platforms will do just fine. However, should you require something specific such as a personalized platform, then you will probably have to pay extra. Try and work with what is readily available rather than finding cool add-ons that may not be necessary at this point in time.

Some platforms are designed for specific financial products like options trading, day trading, currency trading, and swing trading, and so on. As a trader, you should find out if a platform is compatible with your trading style. Therefore, always have the product in mind. Geography is also a consideration is come cases because some platforms are only available to traders in certain jurisdictions and not others.

An Introduction to Fundamental and Technical Analysis

Fundamental Analysis

Fundamental analysis can be defined as the examination, investigation, and research into the underlying factors that closely affect the financial health, success, and wellbeing of companies, industries, and the general economy.

It is a technique used by traders and investors to make a determination regarding the value of a stock or any other financial instrument by examining the factors that directly and indirectly affect a company's or industry's current and future business, financial, economic prospects.

At its most generic form, fundamental analysis endeavors to predict and learn the intrinsic value of securities such as stocks. An in-depth examination and analysis of certain financial, economic, quantitative, and qualitative factors will help in providing the solution.

Fundamental analysis is mostly performed on a company, so a trader can determine whether or not to deal with its stocks. However, it can also be performed on the general economy and on particular industries such as the motor industry, energy sector, and so on.

Fundamental analysis is mostly conducted at the company level because traders and investors are mostly interested in information that will enable them to make a decision at the markets. They want information that will guide them in selecting the most suitable stocks to trade at the markets. As such, traders and investors searching for stocks to trade will resort to examining the competition, a company's business concept, its management, and financial data.

For a proper forecast regarding future stock prices, a trader is required to take into consideration a company's analysis, industry analysis, and even the overall economic outlook. This way, a trader will be able to determine the latest stock price as well as predicted future stock prices. When the outcome of fundamental analysis is not equal to the current market price, then it means that the stock is overpriced or perhaps even undervalued.

Stock analysis can be defined as the process used by traders and investors to acquire in-depth information about a stock or company. The analysis is done by evaluating and studying current and past data about the stock or even the company. This way, traders and investors are able to gain a significant edge in the market as they will be in a position to make well-informed decisions.

Technical Analysis

The term technical analysis is the analysis of past market data, including both volume and price. This is done in order to obtain information that helps in predicting expected market behavior. Traders and investors believe strongly that precious stock price is a reliable indicator of future performance.

There is a notion that supports technical analysis. Apparently, selling and purchase of stocks at the markets collectively by traders, investors, and other players is accurately manifested in the security. This holds then that technical analysis provides a fair and relative accurate market price to a stock or any other security.

Purpose of Technical Analysis

The main purpose of technical analysis is to foretell the expected price movements of stocks and trends and to provide relevant information to investors, traders, and other market players so they can trade profitably.

As a swing trader, you will apply technical analysis to the various charts that you will be using. You will use different tools on the charts so as to determine what the potential entry and exit points for a particular trade are.

Technical analysis can be applied to numerous securities, including Forex, stocks, futures, commodities, indices, and many more. The price of a security depends on a collection of metrics. These are volume, low, open, high, close, open interest, and so on. These are also known as market action or price data.

There are a couple of assumptions that we make as traders when performing technical analysis. However, remember that it is applicable only in situations where the price is only a factor of demand and supply. Should there be other factors that can influence prices significantly, then the technical analysis will not work. The following assumptions are often made about securities that are being analyzed.

Assumptions

Technical analysis assumes that there are no artificial price movements and that past performance is a strong indicator of future price action. Another assumption is that the stocks being analyzed are very liquid. When stocks are heavily traded as a result of liquidity and volume, then traders are able to easily enter and exit trades.

Stocks that are not highly traded tend to be rather difficult to trade because there are very few sellers and buyers at any point in time. Also, stocks with low liquidity are usually poorly priced, sometimes at less than a penny for each share. This is risky as they can be manipulated by investors.

Learn How to Read Charts

As a stock trader, you need to learn how to read charts and to interpret the information obtained from the charts into actionable information. There are numerous types of stock charts. Examples of these charts include candlestick charts, line charts, point-and-figure, open-high-low-close charts, bar charts, and many others. These charts are viewable in varying time frames. For instance, we have weekly, daily, intraday, and even monthly charts.

There advantages and downsides of each chart type and time frame. They find application in different situations. What they reveal include price and volume action, which are extremely important to traders and investors.

Chapter 6: Money Management

As a trader, you have to develop certain skills, and one of these is money management. Learning how to trade is important, but money management is equally important. Money management is simply all about keeping as much of your money as possible and not losing any of it unnecessarily.

As a trader, you do not have any control over the markets, but you can control your money and reduce your losses and any wastage. Money management is just as important as your trading skills. No matter how impressive and on-point your trading skills are, without money management skills, you will not thrive and will be a huge risk. Therefore, learn and understand all the essential aspects of money management.

The main purpose of money management is to ensure that each risk you take is a calculated risk and not guesswork. Every move that you make on the trading platform should be well researched, well informed, and guided by your analysis. Never make any guesswork or blind moves as you risk losing your money. It is better to hold out a little longer from entering a trade rather than lose money blindly.

As the experts say, the key to winning at the stock market losing as little money as possible in the event that you are not right. Some of the key considerations that you should make as a trader are the number of shares you should buy and the amounts to spend per trade.

Candlestick Formation

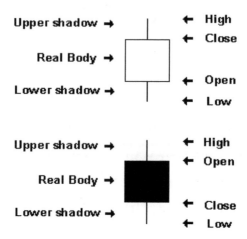

Importance of Proper Money Management Skills

As a trader, one of the most important skills you will need to develop is how to manage your money properly and how to keep as much of it as possible. You need to learn how to save as much of your money as possible and avoid entering trades where you risk losing money. If you are unsure about a strategy, then do not implement it.

Your most crucial goal as a trader should be to preserve and protect your trading capital. This will enable you to last longer and grow your wealth and make big wins. For instance, there is a general rule that you should never spend more than 2% of your trading capital on a single trade. This means that if your trading capital is $100, 000 then no single trade should take more than $2,000. This way, should things not work in your favor, then you stand to lose as little as possible.

Also, no matter how enticing or attractive a position seems, never place a larger amount than initially planned. Market positions on charts sometimes seem way too attractive, and we are inclined to invest more money for higher returns. However, the markets can be unpredictable, and chances of losing money or trades not working out as desired are always high. Therefore, avoid such temptations and stick to your trading plan.

Also, check your account balance each month and then work out the amount that makes 2% of the total. For instance, if your account balance is $50,000, then 2% is equivalent to $1,000. As a swing trader, you cannot afford to lose more than this amount. This kind of approach will enable you to hold onto most of your money as well as stay safe even as you trade. Keep in mind that the premise of the swing trading strategy is to collect profits on half of each position's amount as soon as the stock moves and gains an amount that is equivalent to the original stop loss.

Maintain Proper Cash Flow Management

Always have a very sound and well-thought-out cash flow process. This is probably one of the most crucial elements of long-term investment planning. It is a very simple approach. All you need to do is to deposit money regularly into your accounts. This money can be used to buy more shares for long-term benefits.

Setting Target and Stops

We can define a stop-loss as the total amount of loss that a trader is willing to incur in a single trade. Beyond the stop-loss point, the trader exits the trade. This is basically meant to prevent further losses by thinking the trade will eventually get some momentum. We also have what is known as a take-profit point. It is at this point that you will collect any profits made and possibly exit a trade. At this point, stock or other security is often very close to the point of resistance. Beyond this point, a reversal in price is likely to take place. Rather than lose money, you should exit the trade. Traders sometimes take profit and let trade continue if it was still making money. Another take-profit point is then plotted. If you have a good run, then you can lock in the profits and let the good run continue.

Always Have a Trading Plan

The single most crucial aspect of your trade should be risk management. Without it, your whole trading life will be in jeopardy. Therefore, start all your trading ventures with a plan that you intend to stick by. Traders have a saying that you should plan your trades and then trade your plan. This means to come up with the best plan possible and then implement it and stick by it. Trade is very similar to war. When it is well planned, it can be won before it is executed.

Some of the best tools you will need as part of your risk management plan are take-profit and stop-loss. Using these two tools, you can plan your trades in advance. You will need to use technical analysis in order to determine these two points. With this information, you should be able to determine the price you are willing to pay as well as the losses you can incur.

Risk Versus Reward

A lot of traders lose a lot of money at the markets for a very simple reason. They do not know about risk management or how to go about it. This mostly happens to beginners or novice traders. Most of them simply learn how to trade, then rush to the markets in the hope of making a kill. Sadly, this is now how things work because account and risk management are not taken into consideration.

Managing risk is just as important as learning how to trade profitably. It is a skill that every trader needs to learn, including beginners and novice traders. As it is, investing hard-earned funds at the markets can be a risky venture. Even with the very best techniques and latest software programs, you can still lose money. Experts also lose money at the markets occasionally. The crucial aspect is that they win a lot more than they lose, so the net equation is profitability.

Since trading is a risky affair, traders should be handsomely compensated for the risks they take. This is where the term risk vs. reward ratio comes in. If you are going to invest your money in a venture that carries some risk, then it is good to understand the nature of the risk. If it is too risky, then you may want to keep away but if not, then perhaps the risk is worth it.

Financial Dashboards

A financial dashboard is a management tool commonly used by swing traders and other traders as well. It is mostly used for a fast comparative analysis of major indicator data visually.

The data is often in the form of trend diagrams that are in series form, usually side-by-side. This tool is among the many useful tools that all traders should have if they need to compare market information fast.

A financial dashboard can accommodate huge amounts of data and organize it in such a way that it is easy to visualize it and make fast decisions based on the visualization. A wide variety of data can be formatted and presented to you as you prepared to trade and even as you trade. You will be able to proceed with more accuracy and make informed decisions.

Major Indicators for Stock Traders

As a stock trader, you will need to use a whole bunch of tools. Most of these tools will help to guide you in your stock trading ventures. Some of the best trading indicators or tools are those that will help in the identification of suitable stocks for trading. They include tools that will enable you to identify best market entry points, management of your market positions, and also for-profit collection and market exit.

Fibonacci Retracement

One of the best tools used by most traders, including swing traders, is the Fibonacci retracement pattern. This pattern is used mostly to identify resistance and support levels. When these support and resistance levels are known, it is possible to determine the reversals and hence, appropriate market entry points.

Stocks generally retrace their path a short while after trending either upwards or downwards. The market entry point is often deemed best as soon as the retracement is over, and the trend is resumed. The retracements are generally measured as percentages. Swing traders usually watch out for the 50% market which is rather significant even though it does not exactly fit in with the Fibonacci pattern. Fibonacci is often at ratios ranging from 23.6% and 38.2% all the way to 61.8%.

Pullbacks

By their very own nature, pullbacks always generate a variety of different trading opportunities after a trend moves lower or higher. Profiting through this classic strategy is not as easy as it sounds. For instance, you may invest in a security or sell short into a resistance position, and these trends can continue so that your losses are considerable. Alternatively, your security or stock could just sit there and waste away even as you miss out on many other opportunities.

There are certain skills you need if you are to earn decent profits with the pullback strategy. For instance, how aggressive should a trader be, and at what point should profit be taken? When is it time to pull out? Basically, these and all other important aspects should be considered.

For starters, you require a strong trend on the markets such that other traders' timing pullbacks get to line up right behind you. When they do, they will cause your idea to become a really profitable one. Securities that ascend to new heights or falling to new lows are capable of attaining this requirement, especially after the securities push much farther beyond the breakout level.

You will also need persistent vertical action into a trough or peak for regular profits, especially if the volumes are higher than usual, mainly because this results in a fast price movement once you attain the position. It is imperative that the stock in question turns a profit quickly after either bottoming or topping out but with no sizable trade range or consolidation. It is also crucial that this happens. Otherwise, the intervening range is likely to oppose profitability during the resulting subsequent rollover or bounce.

Resistance and Support Triggers

There are lines known as support and resistance points that form the core of the technical analysis. It is easy to build a trading plan using these indicators. The first one is the support line, and it is a good indicator of the price level. It also indicates areas below prevailing market prices on the chart with strong buying pressure.

Resistance levels or points are the exact opposite of the support levels. Resistance lines are a clear representation of an area or price levels that are over and above the prevailing market prices, and selling pressure does overcome any buying pressure. As a swing trader, you will enter a position off the resistance level then place a stop loss point just above the clearly defined resistance level.

Candlestick Patterns

Traders also use candlestick patterns as part of their analysis. We can have a single candlestick or a combination of two or even three. Candlesticks are widely used indicators that enable us to observe potential trend reversals and market direction changes. Candlesticks are formed based on the price action in a given period of time. For instance, if we have a candlestick based out of a 5-minute chart, then it will demonstrate the price action for the specific 5-minute period. The same is true for the 1-hour and even 4-hour time periods.

Moving Averages

The best way to identify these two crucial points is to use moving averages. The reason why we prefer moving averages to determine the stop-loss and take-profit points. These are closely tracked by the markets and very simple to determine. Some of the popular moving averages include the 5-day, 20-day, 50-day, 100-day, and 200-day averages. Simply apply these to your security's chart then make a determination about the best points.

You can also use support and resistance lines to determine the take-profit and stop-loss points. This is also a pretty simple process. Simply connect past lows and highs that happened in the recent past on key, high-than-normal volume levels. They work on the same principle as the moving averages. All that you need to do is to find levels where the price action will respond to the trend line on areas of high volume.

Identifying Swings

The market is constantly in motion. A swing occurs when there are two consecutive lower highs and lower lows or when there are two consecutive higher lows and higher highs. Remember that swings appear in all manner of shapes and sizes. However, the rule on how to identify them is very simple. Simply look for consecutive higher highs and higher lows or consecutive lower highs and lower lows.

Swings are bullish if the general movement is upwards and bearish if the general movement is downwards. Sometimes a new low will appear when the trend is upwards. At other times a new high will appear when the general trend is headed downwards. When this happens, you should not be worried or concerned as these are considered false swings. Unless there are consecutive highs or lows, then ignore everything else.

Accounting Software

It is advisable to get appropriate accounting software for use with your trading activities. There is always money entering and leaving your account. It is important to keep a proper tab on your costs and expenses as well as track your profits and perhaps even losses.

There are numerous accounting software packages available. These vary from one provider to the next. The most crucial aspect is whether they can perform the tasks that you need to perform. For instance, how much trading capital did you start off with? You may want to keep an eye on this and see if it is growing based on your approach.

You also want to keep track of your costs and profits. You will enter some of these figures in your trading journal as well. Therefore, search for accounting software that is easy to use, which provides you with the information that you need and also software that can integrate with your trading platform.

Watching your money is extremely important as a trader. Your aim is to watch your money and keep an eye on your profits and expenditure. Any prudent trader needs to do this. With a good financial accounting system in place, you will be able to trade successfully and watch your expenses and income. Should any remedial action become necessary, then you will note that through your accounting and take action especially in lowering costs or raising revenues.

Why You Need a Trade Journal

As a swing trader, you need to keep a journal so that you have a reliable record of your trades and their performance. This is one of the best ways of learning about your style and performance. Trade tracking journals also enables you to track your trades and the actions you took during certain situations and instances. In short, a trading journal provides traders with the necessary tools and information that they need to evaluate their trading activities objectively.

As a trader, you really should be tracking your trades throughout the day. A journal helps you to keep a record of the happenings each day, as well as your reactions or actions. Your plan should include a tried and tested system that suits your trading style.

Make sure that you test this system and review it often then improve your trading plans and performance.

Poor trading systems do not necessarily cause failure or bad performance. Most traders lose out and incur losses simply because they do not adhere to the rules of their preferred trading system. Many lose out because they cannot keep track of their trading plan. This is where a trade journal comes in handy.

If you have a serious trading plan, then a journal will help you to adhere to this trading plan. By following your well laid out plan, you will have much better chances of success. It is important to keep the journal as detailed as possible. Here are some of the ways you can make your journal as thorough as possible. This is important as your journal is only as good as the information it contains.

First, you need to ensure that that you are honest with the information you enter and as thorough as possible. It beats the purpose is the information provided is not accurate and honest because it will be of very little benefit to you. Also, you should learn how to enter information and data into a trading journal and how to maintain it appropriately. This way, you will become a disciplined trader.

Also, with time, you should begin reflecting on your journal entries. When you do this, you will learn a lot about yourself, and you will improve your trading skills immensely. You also get to track your thoughts and trades the entire trading day.

Managing a Trading Journal

A trading journal contains useful information and relevant details that you receive from your broker as your trading performance. You will get to learn more about market conditions prevalent during your trading experiences. If you made any mistakes as you were trading or got distracted somewhat, then the journal will be able to keep track of any errors and mistakes. You can also put down any trading strategy that may come up in the course of trading.

Ensure that you put down as much detail as possible. For instance, remember to include the prevailing market conditions at the time the trade was underway. The entries will open up your eyes to plenty of things that traders miss as they trade. A journal may not be so crucial to a day trader but is definitely recommended for all swing traders.

It is advisable to note that there is no need to actually take a pen and notebook and physically enter every minute detail that occurs. Instead, you can use other preferred methods. For instance, we could use regular screen captures to take a picture of the trading platform as the trade progresses.

Other swing traders prefer to add notes, marks, and annotations to their trading charts in the course of the trading day. They mark indicator levels and draw lines. These actions are useful in a number of ways and can help in determining the direction of the trend. It also helps when it comes to identifying possible entry points and reversal points. Charts indicate the exact market conditions during the entire trading day. Many find it easy to keep pictures of different instances of the trading day. However, notes here and there, marks, and annotations help to make things clear.

Conclusion

Thank you for making it through to the end of *Swing Trading*, let's hope it was informative and able to provide you with all of the tools you need to achieve your goals whatever they may be.

The next step is to begin practicing swing trading on paper and investigating the strategies even closer. Learning theory is one tiny aspect. Putting all your knowledge to practice and sharpening your trading acumen is crucial. You only become an excellent trader by going live and trading on an actual platform, even if it is just a virtual one.

You also need to learn as much as possible about money and risk management. Even with excellent trading skills, you will not be a successful swing trader unless you learn how to keep your money safe and avoid unnecessary losses or wastage. All too often, a novice trader will forget about their skills when trading live on a real platform. This will cause them to lose money, and they will probably eventually quit. Good money management techniques are the hallmark of any great trader.